"I don't know if you struggle with loneliness, but I used to. And honestly, I wish I'd had this book back then. I think it would have been a great help and given me some tangible things I could do to combat the feeling of solitude, of not fitting in. Because I'm married to the guy, I know Jack's heart and his desire to see people connected—not just to one another but to Jesus. I highly recommend this book for all ages in all walks of life. You won't be sorry you read it. In fact, you might find yourself seeing others in a new light and reaching out to offer friendship and hope to someone who has none. Take the time to read the book, then go be the one who brings a smile to a lonely person's face and a renewing of joy to their heart."

Lynette Eason, bestselling and award-winning author of over fifty books, including the Danger Never Sleeps series

"Years ago, a well-known megachurch pastor told me, 'Loneliness is the hardest part of my ministry.' He speaks for thousands of ministry leaders and other Christians who struggle with this same dilemma: so many people, so few meaningful relationships. This book lays out the problem, along with practical solutions for solving the loneliness dilemma. If you feel isolated and disconnected, this book will be a lifeline of hope for you."

Jeff Iorg, president of Gateway Seminary

"This wonderful book shows the heart of this friend of mine in so many ways. It flows freely from the depth of his real-life experience and deals with the issues we all grapple with as we live out the reality of this life God has given us. Jack speaks truth and provides one practical application after another in an effort to encourage and guide every reader. I wholeheartedly recommend you read this and then pass it along. Too many of us need to know we are, in fact, better together!"

Don Wilton, pastor of First Baptist Church, Spartanburg, South Carolina (Dr. Billy Graham's former pastor)

"I strongly recommend this timely and needed book. Jack Eason exposes why the most interconnected and overconnected generations in history self-identify as the loneliest. He doesn't leave it as simply a description of a state of being but rather reveals God's solution. With engaging and relatable stories, Eason expresses God's desire that man or woman not be alone, and he provides practical, biblical steps to remedy the issue. Each chapter concludes with a list of recommended action steps. This is more than a theoretical treatise; it's a call to action in the community and, as revealed in the final chapters, even within the church."

David Tarkington, pastor of First Baptist Church of Orange Park, Florida, and founder of First Family Network

"We have never had more 'friends' yet been lonelier than we are in our current culture. Social media isn't the answer to this pervasive loneliness and desire for inspiration and genuine relationships. Jack Eason provides a captivating narrative directing readers to the hope and answer for loneliness found only in a relationship with Jesus Christ."

Rick Brewer, president and professor of management, Louisiana College

"*I'm lonely* are two of the most vulnerable, and yes, lonesome, words we can speak. To speak them can deepen our loneliness by putting us in touch with our private fear that we are weak, needy, and unworthy. Enter Pastor Jack Eason. Written for leaders, lay people, and those simply wrestling with their own personal sense of isolation, *The Loneliness Solution* is a deeply compassionate book that shines a warm light into the dark, solitary confinement of loneliness. Jack Eason has given us a book that offers companionship to the reader while equipping them to recognize and address the problem of loneliness in ourselves and in those around us."

Jason Gray, recording artist/songwriter

The
Loneliness
Solution

The Loneliness Solution

Finding Meaningful Connection

in a Disconnected World

Jack Eason

Revell

a division of Baker Publishing Group
Grand Rapids, Michigan

Published by Revell
a division of Baker Publishing Group
PO Box 6287, Grand Rapids, MI 49516-6287
www.revellbooks.com

Printed in the United States of America

Library of Congress Cataloging-in-Publication Data
Names: Eason, Jack, 1965– author.
Title: The loneliness solution : finding meaningful connection in a disconnected world / Jack Eason.
Description: Grand Rapids, Michigan : Revell, a division of Baker Publishing Group, 2020.
Identifiers: LCCN 2020014697 | ISBN 9780800737894 (paperback) | ISBN 9780800739911 (casebound)
Subjects: LCSH: Loneliness—Religious aspects—Christianity.
Classification: LCC BV4911 .E26 2020 | DDC 248.8/6—dc23
LC record available at https://lccn.loc.gov/2020014697

In keeping with biblical principles of creation stewardship, Baker Publishing Group advocates the responsible use of our natural resources. As a member of the Green Press Initiative, our company uses recycled paper when possible. The text paper of this book is composed in part of post-consumer waste.

20 21 22 23 24 25 26   7 6 5 4 3 2 1

green press
INITIATIVE

How could I not dedicate my first published book
to my inspiration for writing?

My wife and published author, Lynette, has encouraged me
for many years to put my thoughts into book form.

Thank you, sweetie. I dedicate this book to you.

Contents

Contents

Acknowledgments

There are many people who inspired me to put these thoughts into print.

I want to thank Lynette Eason for her nonstop encouragement to write, as well as the support of Will and Lauryn and my entire family.

Thanks especially to Tamela Hancock Murray and the Steve Laube Agency for believing in me and the ideas for this book.

A special appreciation for Vicki Crumpton and the entire team at Revell for helping me address a much-needed topic that people around the world are dealing with.

I also give appreciation to the many people who have been patient with my schedule to get this book accomplished and have helped in some way with time or talent: Tammy Markheim, Abby Scull, and the Crossover CUPS Team, as well as my Cross Roads church family.

Huge kudos go to Andrew Jackson, James Way, and Jeremy Powers for the technology helps in this book. For many of the stories you will find in the book, you will find a podcast available of the full interview at JackEason.org.

Much applause goes to people who are great at encouraging relationships and connectivity: Mike Williams, Brian Smith, Bill Sammons.

Many thanks to the ministries I get to serve each year who trust me to encourage their partners with the message of this book—that we are all important and need to be connected with each other. We are better together.

PART ONE

The Problem of Loneliness

CHAPTER ONE

Living Life Alone

> Loneliness and the feeling of being unwanted is the most terrible poverty.
>
> Mother Teresa

Loneliness is killing us, and we don't even realize it.

The internet and social media give us the illusion that we're more connected than ever before. Advancements in technology have made it possible for us to communicate in real time across oceans, cultures, and continents—and even to outer space. Because of technology, we can see the people we are talking to on screens we hold in our hands. With networks that are supposed to be "social," we can add and subtract friends at will with a mouse click.

The appearance of connection makes us think we are doing life with others, but let's be honest. Many of those "friends" are merely acquaintances. We don't really know our friends on social networks. For sure, we would never meet up with them IRL (in real life). Sometimes we feel more or less important based on the number of friends we have in those networks. We call all this technology "progress," but is it? Perhaps it has made us more insulated and isolated. And that should concern us. This connection illusion can have catastrophic consequences.

Loneliness Kills

How does loneliness kill? Recently, I read an article that horrified me.[1] He was only fifty-four years of age and had worked at companies such as Nissan and Fujitsu. Yet the gray-haired man who parted his hair in the middle, wore wire-frame glasses, and was a fan of checkered shirts was gone. When they found him, he'd been dead for four months. **Four months.**

As winter slowly turned to spring, the smell from his apartment caught the attention of neighbors.

A leader of the crew from Next, a company that specializes in cleaning up after "lonely deaths," was part of the initial discovery team. Did you catch that? An entire company that cleans up lonely deaths. How would you like to work for *that* company?

The team leader said he sees this all the time. NLI Research Institute, a Tokyo think tank, estimates that about thirty thousand people nationwide die this way each year.[2] *Alone.* Though this story took place in Japan, many predict lonely deaths will become more commonplace across the globe unless something changes.

Did you read that? They will become *more commonplace.*

Statistics indicate that more and more people are feeling lonely. We are a naturally social people *made* to interact with one another. Yet without conscious effort, our way of life reduces real quality in our relationships. An American Psychological Association study concluded that lonely people are at a greater risk for premature death.[3] Lonely people die early.

Researchers found that people with fewer social relationships die sooner than those with more. The study also found that the influence of the lack of relationships is comparable with well-established risk factors for mortality such as smoking and drinking, and even exceeds the risks of physical inactivity and obesity. These studies of elderly people and social isolation concluded that those without adequate social interaction were twice as likely to die prematurely. Unbelievable!

A study by leading health industry experts from Cigna, surveying twenty thousand people, found the following:

- Only around half of Americans (53 percent) say they have meaningful, daily face-to-face social interactions, including an extended conversation with a friend or spending quality time with family.
- Members of Generation Z (adults aged eighteen to twenty-two for the purposes of this study) say they are the loneliest generation and claim to be in worse health than older generations. And yet they seem to be more connected than any generation in the history of the world.
- Social media use alone is not a predictor of loneliness, as heavy users have a loneliness score (43.5) that is only slightly higher than people who say they never use social media (41.7).[4]

The number of people you know doesn't matter. Whether you know only real-life people or have five-thousand-plus friends on Facebook, you can still feel alone. Our inner circle should consist of people with whom we can build trust and confidence. But have our social media "relationships" encouraged us to settle for less than what real relationships can give us? Have we replaced the real and rich relationships we were created for with the false shrines of Twitter and Instagram?

Medical experts and political leaders are becoming increasingly worried about the problem of loneliness. Strategies are being launched all over the globe to fight it. In October 2017, a former surgeon general of the United States, Vivek Murthy, called loneliness an "epidemic."[5] In January 2017, former British prime minister Theresa May appointed a "minister of loneliness."[6] Unless we find a solution for loneliness, some real trouble could be in store.

Loneliness Defined

We know the problem of loneliness exists, but how do we measure it? We can assess a problem like obesity because we can quantify it by numbers on a scale or by a body mass index score. It is measurable. How do we measure an emotion? Can we use a 1–10 scale? And if so, what number marks the need for intervention? Seven? Eight?

The experts studying this growing problem define loneliness as "**perceived** social isolation, a feeling of not having the social contacts one would like."[7] Of course, those who are isolated are much more likely to feel lonely. But loneliness can also affect those who seemingly have a large group of friends or family members. So loneliness is not limited to places on the globe that are less technologically advanced, where social networks may be fewer.

Loneliness Knows No Geographical Barriers

In fact, *The Economist* and the Kaiser Family Foundation, a non-profit group that focuses on health, partnered together to survey people in the wealthy countries of America, Britain, and Japan. The study revealed that 9 percent of adults in Japan, 22 percent in America, and 23 percent in Britain always or often feel lonely, lack true companionship, or feel left out or isolated.[8]

These findings, unfortunately, are not surprising. They are similar to what a University of Southern California, Los Angeles, study found. The study used statements such as "I have nobody to talk to" and "I find myself waiting for people to call or write." Respondents indicated to what extent they agreed or disagreed with each statement. Those people who scored above a certain number were categorized as being "lonely."

As I researched this book, I have to admit that I began to be overwhelmed. I have felt for the last several years that loneliness is a growing issue, and what I learned confirmed that.

A 2010 study estimated that "35% of Americans over 45 were lonely. Of these, 45% had felt this way for at least six years; a further 32% for one to five years." Britain's Office for National Statistics (ONS) asked a simple question in 2013 and classified "25% of people aged 52 or over as 'sometimes lonely,' with an extra 9% 'often lonely.'" Age UK, a charity in Britain, found 41 percent of seniors say that television or a pet "is their main source of company." And in Japan, "*more than half a million people* stay at home for at least six months at a time, making no contact with the outside world, according to a report by the government in 2016." And statistics like this are showing up for countries all over the globe.[9]

Are isolation and loneliness connected? Data tends to support this. "Isolation does seem to be increasing, so loneliness may be too."[10] Look how many people are living alone. Solo households are on the rise, and many are opting to live alone as a sign of independence.

Other indicators confirm the problem:

Isolation is increasing in other ways, too. From 1985 to 2009 the average size of an American's social network—defined by number of confidants—declined by more than one-third. Other studies suggest that fewer Americans join in social communities like church groups or sports teams.

Only recently has medicine studied the links between relationships and health. Julianne Holt-Lunstad of Brigham Young University finished a project in 2015 that studied 3.4 million participants who were followed over an average of seven years. Holt-Lunstad found that those categorized as lonely had a 26% higher risk of dying, and those living alone a 32% higher chance, after accounting for differences in age and health status.[11]

Loneliness among the Elderly

"Having a partner seems especially important for older people, as generally they have fewer (but often closer) relationships than the young do."[12]

Consider Ana's story. Ana lives in a house full of rooms she never goes into. "It's the home she grew up in with her parents and four siblings, and where she later brought up her own children and looked after her husband. Now, the two-story house is too big for her," but it's too painful for her to let go of it. "'My husband died. My daughters got married and went to work abroad. I was left on my own.'"[13] This may imply that a common reason for loneliness among the elderly is that they have lost their partner.

Ana's been on her own for thirteen years—that's "a lot of time and a lot of empty space for this eighty-year-old woman." Most of her time is spent in the living room, where she can look through tons of old photos. "She says she lives more in the past than in the present."[14] Most of the time she doesn't even realize what day of the week it is.

Unfortunately, based on studies, loneliness among the elderly will continue to rise as the population reaches historic proportions. "The world's older population continues to grow at an unprecedented rate. Today, 8.5 percent of people worldwide (617 million) are aged 65 and over." According to a recent report, "this percentage is projected to jump to nearly 17 percent of the world's population by 2050 (1.6 billion)."[15]

Loneliness among the Young

Loneliness is not limited to the elderly. The Holt-Lunstad study found "no clear link between age and loneliness in America or Britain— and in Japan younger people were in fact lonelier. Young adults, and the very old (over-85s, say) tend to have the highest percentages of lonely people of any adult age-group. Other research suggests that, among the elderly, loneliness tends to have a specific cause, such as widowhood." In the young, loneliness tends to relate to "a gap in expectations between relationships they have and those they want."[16]

> According to a recent survey . . . , the loneliest generation in the United States today is not the oldest Americans but the youngest, specifically young adults between 18 and 22 years old.[17]

Take, for example, *Daphne Armstrong*. Daphne, who's from the heart of Missouri, remembers when she first came to the University of Southern California (USC) in Los Angeles and felt a bit out of place in the big city.

"There was some culture shock," said Armstrong, who is now a junior. "All my roommates were from [Southern California] and grew up going to USC football games and seemed already so involved in the community."[18]

To feel more at home, she began FaceTiming her family every day, calling her mom, her dad, and her sister.

> "I was always texting and chatting with my friend groups back home instead of putting time and energy into people around me," she said.
>
> Feeling alone at college—especially freshman year—is nothing new.

"A certain amount of this is to be expected," said the Rev. Jim Burklo, associate dean of the Office of Religious Life at USC. "You don't know anyone and you're starting from scratch."

But USC officials—and officials across the country—are noticing that technology and social media are making connectedness even harder. Burklo and others started talking about a "loneliness epidemic" on campus . . . and the United States has labeled it a public health concern in need of intervention.[19]

While loneliness is a common issue among college students, the causes are not what you might expect. For instance, it is not always the lack of people that makes a student feel lonely, but the lack of *quality interactions*, or connections. In fact, it is not uncommon for college students to report that they feel lonely at college despite being in a crowd of people they know and with whom they spend time. So, loneliness and being alone are **not** the same thing.

So, why, exactly, is loneliness bad for our health? Dolores Malaspina, professor of psychiatry, neuroscience, and genetics at the Icahn School of Medicine at Mount Sinai in New York, says, "Humans are a social species with an innate biological drive to connect. . . . Human survival depends on connectedness, with feelings of loneliness serving as a biological signal to socialize."[20]

People are lonely everywhere, even when they are not alone. Just being in the presence of other people does not guarantee you won't be lonely. And there seem to be a few factors that can lead us to being lonely.

Factors in Loneliness

What seem to be some of the issues that surround isolation and loneliness? There are a few possibilities that Quentin Fottrell shares. [21] See if any of these fit you. This is not meant to be an exhaustive list, but it's a good start to get us thinking.

Social media. Social media can be beneficial when it's used appropriately and sparingly. But a report in the *American Journal of Preventive Medicine* found this: People who spent the most time on social media had twice the odds of having greater perceived social isolation, according to a 2017 study of more than 1,700 people.[22] If you have an iPhone, check the "screen time" option to see how much you are looking at your screen. I did, and my stats shocked me into making some real changes.

Dependence on prescription drugs. "People are being overprescribed drugs to deal with both physical and emotional problems. In a [*Consumer Reports*] survey released last year of 1,947 American adults, more than 50% said they regularly take prescription medications. . . . The total number of prescriptions filled for adults and children in the US increased by 85% from 1997 to 2016, while the US population only increased by 21% in the same period."[23] That's astounding.

Replacing substance with stuff. Our consumer culture doesn't help. When people get sick of their routine, and life seems purposeless, then people do get depressed, even with many physical comforts. Sometimes that depression feeds isolation, and then we consume more stuff, thinking it will make us happy and no longer lonely. This includes material possessions as well as consuming things like food.

Overwork. This is especially true for the Gen X population. Because inflation has outpaced income, many of them are working longer hours or two jobs just to keep their heads above water. All that work means less time for friends, family, or other interactions with people. So, it's work and sleep, and sleep and work.

This list doesn't cover all the possibilities, but it's a great start in pinpointing the reality of loneliness. And hopefully, it gets us asking questions like these: How do we move out of loneliness and into friendships? What obstacles keep us from real friendships and the benefits of doing life with others? As we figure out the challenges to doing life together, we move toward the solution to loneliness.

PRACTICAL QUESTIONS TO CONSIDER

1. How do you define loneliness? How is it different from being alone? Describe a time when you were alone and a time when you were lonely.

   _____

   _____

   _____

2. Why do you think people are so isolated from one another?

   _____

   _____

   _____

3. Describe a situation you know of where someone was living life alone and the result was not a good one.

   _____

   _____

   _____

PUT IT INTO PRACTICE

Today as you go through your daily tasks, make a conscious effort to observe people. Who do you see that appears to be lonely? Are they all alone? Do you see anyone in a group who appears to still be lonely? Attempt to watch both those who are older and some who are younger to see if there are any differences that you pick up on between the two groups.

CHAPTER TWO

It's Hard to Find Someone to Talk To

Have you ever thought about what the first *problem* in the world was? It was not sin, but solitude.

Drew Hunter

I just finished watching *Creed II*. I'm partial to the Rocky movies of my childhood, but Sylvester Stallone was smart and savvy to continue the heroic boxing story for the next generation. *Creed*'s Adonis received the same instruction that Rocky himself received from his manager when he was being pummeled in the ring. After wiping his bleeding brow and spraying some water in his mouth, Rocky tells the young Adonis, "Get back out there and finish the fight!"

Maybe because I am a guy, I like that imagery. But all of us feel from time to time like life is beating us up. And what helps me is to have someone who cares enough to encourage me and send me back out to face another day. For me, it describes the essence of a healthy relationship. A place to be vulnerable. A place to receive healing. A place to be encouraged to get back in the fight.

Why Is It So Hard?

Even if we know we're missing something, we still all have things that get in the way of relationships. I've tried to find real, authentic relationships in many groups over the years. Many times, I wanted to throw up my hands in the air, put my ear pods in, and just let the music keep me company. But that's giving up too easily. When we identify the obstacles that are keeping us from making authentic connections, then we can overcome them.

Things That Get in the Way of Relationships

Independence. We value our independence. We brag about our independence. We even have a day to celebrate it. As a father, I take pride in my children showing their independence as they get older. From the time they cry, "Mine!" as a toddler to them "testing the waters" in their teenage years, every step of growth moves toward independence. Every parent I know wants to raise their children to be independent, productive citizens. No one wants a child living in the basement at thirty-five, right? But perhaps we've gone a little too far with that. I wonder if this idea of independence has devolved into us thinking we are weak creatures if we admit our need for others. Independence is the attitude that I don't need anyone else.

A friend remarked recently that the designs of our homes have changed over the years into spaces that limit relationships and community. My grandmother's house had a huge front porch with a big swing that we used to enjoy. We'd hang out on that front

26

porch in the evenings, knowing someone would eventually "drop by," and we would congregate on the front porch to have conversation and cultivate relationships. My, how times have changed. Large front porches are rare today. And the furniture in our living rooms faces in one direction: toward the television.

We are better together than apart. And when we choose to be **interdependent instead of independent**, we allow each person in a relationship to show self-expression. What do I mean by this? Simply that each one of us has a unique mix of gifts, passions, abilities, personalities, and experiences. We all have an irrepressible desire to express our uniqueness. When we're unable to do that, frustration, dissatisfaction, and boredom result. We each have unique strengths and talents. When we're so independent that we don't "need" anyone else, we prevent other people from sharing their gifts with us. Likewise, we have fewer opportunities to share our talents with others. We can be so independent that we can snuff out the uniqueness of others. So be careful of the attitude of independence. When it's done right, it's a good thing. Taken to the extreme, it's a big obstacle to doing life with others.

Busyness. For the overachievers (and technology has helped us all think this way), it's what we get done each day that makes us feel important. We've all gotten the impression that our value is based on the number of things we have on our to-do list, and that keeps us from relationships. "Sorry, I can't have lunch . . . I'm busy."

We turn down the opportunity to connect with someone because we have decided that checking off another item on our task list is more important. This wrong thinking will lead to continual behaviors that will push us away from conversation and community.

Technology. Technology has revolutionized the way we connect with one another. Dan Doriani's *The New Man: Becoming a Man After God's Heart* says this about technology and mobility: "Mobility is part of the culture of freedom that Americans treasure, but it destroys friendships by severing the regular contact friends need. It ends the joyful retelling of shared triumphs and sorrows—the tales of the unbearable boss, the impossible task accomplished. Mobility separates friends, and men recover slowly because they hardly try to recover. Mobility encourages rootlessness. As we haul up the anchors of family, history, and tradition, we become vulnerable to the call to reinvent ourselves."[1] How true! Our storytelling has now devolved into one or two text messages with emojis thrown in for effect. Text messages and "likes" will never take the place of face-to-face communication.

My daughter, Lauryn, recently returned from studying abroad. She experienced so many incredible things and posted a lot of pictures on Facebook and Instagram. Although I followed her on social media, I longed to see her face-to-face to hear the stories behind those pictures and videos I was seeing. I wanted to hear the details of the events unfolding in the Twittersphere. Unfortunately, a lot of us have substituted this quick yet perhaps incomplete method of sharing for that in-person communication that is so vital to our souls. I wanted to see her facial expressions and sense her body language as she shared the experiences of a lifetime.

Pride. Whether we admit it or not, we are all capable of being prideful. As soon as we say, "I'm not proud," we become so. Because of our humanity, not to mention the influence of our culture, our hearts are oftentimes seeking to lift **us** up, and to make much of us. The culture around us pressures us into "looking out for number one." Doing life together (which should be about building up others) and pride are incompatible. They push us in different directions. Pride can harm us because it blinds us. But it also keeps us from life-giving relationships with other people. No one likes someone who is all about themselves. Pride is the attitude that I am better than everyone else.

Have you ever been in a conversation with someone only to feel like they couldn't care less about what you had to say? More and more that seems to be the norm in our society, because we have forgotten how to talk to people. Thus, there is little value placed on genuine conversation.

Could you possibly be prideful and sustain any kind of meaningful relationship with another human being? Of course not. The prideful person never apologizes, never admits wrongdoing, and always puts their own needs before the needs of others. You probably know someone like this. But have you ever been like this? Unfortunately, I have to confess that I have. I also know people who've been like this. When we acknowledge pride, we have taken the first step to overcoming it. And it's an obstacle that has to be overcome if we are going to be able to do life with others.

The delusion of self-sufficiency. All of us have the tendency to think that we know more than we actually do. We believe that we are self-sufficient and in need of no one else, but nothing could be further from the truth. The real truth is that we depend on God for every breath that we take. We were created with the need to walk through life with other people. If we believe that we are self-sufficient, we don't see a need for people. When this happens, we fail to see a reason to invest the time it takes to build relationships with others.

But the opposite is true as well, right? Many of us feel like we have nothing to offer. Perhaps we think that nobody really wants to be our friend. We may even ask the question, "Why would they want to have me as a friend?"

Maybe we think something in our past or in our makeup prevents us from being "qualified" for acceptance as a friend for someone else. But that's not true. Each of us has something of value that will enhance friendship with another person.

Compartments. Have you noticed all the new labels we've created for people? Divisions. Specializations. Whatever you want to call it. There's a whole myriad of distinctions just for people's gender and sexual preference. While we might think we are giving power and recognition to these groups of people, we may be increasingly segregating them and ourselves by placing them into different compartments, creating more isolation from one another. Add to this a hypersensitive and divisive political landscape and the walls that separate us seem to grow higher by the hour.

My point is, when we concentrate on our differences more than our similarities, it will be difficult to find something that connects us to one another. At the end of the day, there is one race, the human race, but we tend to forget that with all the division we have created in our effort to celebrate individualism. Let's commit to look for things we have in common with others, no matter how much labels try to divide us.

The disconnection of the family. When I was growing up, we had reunions with extended family. Often, there would be forty to fifty people who would gather. Just a few decades later, we find ourselves struggling to get together with our immediate family. And because of the erosion of the family, many people have no one they can call family. This is an epidemic and a contributor to the issue of loneliness.

One of the joys of family is hand-me-downs. I'm not talking about clothes, though I got a lot of those growing up. I'm talking about the passing down of traditions, lessons, and stories that comes from strong family connection. We are losing that in our society, and with it we lose wisdom and understanding that would help us communicate more effectively with one another.

So how do we overcome these obstacles? How do we kiss pride goodbye and free ourselves from the delusion of things like self-sufficiency? Maybe we start by taking a risk.

A Simple Lesson on *Risk*

A while back, I went to a conference in Washington, DC. I didn't stay at the overly expensive hotel where the conference was held.

Rather, I opted for a wonderful little rental house just a short walk away. Because of that experience, I learned something about relationships from a company simply known as Airbnb.

At the core of our relationships is *taking a risk to be vulnerable with someone so connection can happen.* What does that have to do with us or Airbnb?

Using Airbnb the first time admittedly took a little bravery. Staying in someone else's home and treating it like you would a hotel felt a little too "out of the box" at first. I wondered if pictures online could be trusted and if my stay would be pleasant. But a friend's personal encouragement—and of course, Yelp testimonials— allowed me to trust enough to make that click the first time.

My place was amazing! It was clean, private, and everything promised in the advertisement. After that first experience, Airbnb became a *trusted* friend. Each trip provided great experiences of meeting new, often *very* interesting, people. The hosts have shared unique things about their city, favorite places they eat, or sights that are a must-see. As a result, choosing Airbnb is easy for me. After repeated pleasant experiences, I'm no longer concerned about booking a stay through the company. Those consistently wonderful interactions have built up a foundation of faith in Airbnb and introduced me to some wonderful people—some with whom I still have relationships.

Airbnb connects people in over 100,000 cities in more than 220 countries.[2] The cofounders decided early on they didn't want to build only a marketplace, they wanted a place for *interactive relationships* between friends and fans. That community, they believed, would build their marketplace. Most marketplaces are built on money, and most businesses are built on money, but the founders knew money would only go so far. They wanted something that would turn into a *movement.*

The currency that Airbnb was built upon was **trust among people** *who did not know each other: the person staying as a guest*

31

in the home, apartment, or townhouse, and the owner-renter of the property. The founders believed that if you create a business based on money, that business will become transactional. Airbnb wanted to build interactions and community because they recognized those things would build Airbnb into the hospitality organization they dreamed it could be. So, they decided that if money is the currency of transactions, then *trust would be the currency of interactions.* They also knew that increased interactions would increase profitability.[3] And they have been absolutely correct.

What can we learn about relationships and togetherness from Airbnb? People are being asked every day to make "trust leaps," especially with more and more technology in our culture. The first time someone used eBay was a trust leap. The first time someone had something delivered by an Amazon drone was a trust leap. The first time someone used Uber was a trust leap. The reality is, these types of things are happening more frequently in society.

I realize, for many of us, connecting with a new person—a person who has had no experience with us—is uncomfortable because so much about them is unknown. And for most people, that's a great chasm to cross. You don't know the person yet, so you aren't going to be comfortable until trust has been established. Basically, you want to trust someone new but fear that trust will be broken while you are getting to know them. That's the challenge. This chasm between the known and the unknown is risk. The bridge that transports people from the unknown to the known is named trust. The pylons that support it are forged from confidence. The architect is known by their history.

The challenge each of us faces is that many places are betraying our trust every day. You don't have to look too far to find a news article or a television report about Social Security numbers being compromised or someone's personal information being stolen. I received a notice yesterday that several thousand students in our county have had their Social Security numbers breached by a computer hacker. Last week, one of my credit card companies reported hackers had accessed their database. Not only that, but let's face it: many groups, even churches, have breached the trust of their members and attendees. Treasurers have embezzled money from their charities. Television pastors have been exposed for living in multimillion-dollar homes while raising money to supposedly help the poor in their communities. Is it any wonder people struggle to trust one another? Is it any wonder people tend not to be as open to sharing personal information as they used to be?

How can we overcome this epidemic of loneliness so many of us experience? What are some solutions our culture is coming up with to help us face this issue? Let's look at some of them in the next chapter.

PRACTICAL QUESTIONS TO CONSIDER

1. What are the obstacles you relate to when it comes to doing life together?

_____

_____

_____

_____

2. Have you overcome any of those obstacles? If so, how?

_____

_____

_____

3. Do you see trust as a challenge in your day-to-day relationships? If so, why do you think the challenge exists?

_____

_____

_____

4. What are some creative ways to develop trust in your relationships?

_____

_____

_____

PUT IT INTO PRACTICE

Take time today to write down some of the things that get in the way of your having relationships. Think about how you can overcome each of the obstacles that you list. If you haven't tried Airbnb, Uber, Lyft, or Amazon, set up an account for one of these services and try it. Then write down how you felt about using it.

CHAPTER THREE

The Fight against Loneliness

> Loneliness is my least favorite thing about life. The thing that I'm most worried about is just being alone without anybody to care for or someone who will care for me.
>
> Anonymous

Stories of loneliness are all around us. I was traveling to Atlanta, Georgia, for a short business trip. Just shy of my destination, my rumbling stomach got the best of me. The Chick-fil-A logo on the exit sign lured me off I-85, and I pulled in for a quick bite. Who can pass up some Chick-fil-A, right?

After ordering and receiving the expected "My pleasure!" I found a seat next to the window and grabbed a waffle fry. I looked across the crowded room and was amazed at what I saw. With the exception of one or two moms with kids in tow, all the other tables were filled with groups of people. But what caught my attention was that at the majority of those tables, no conversation was taking place. People ate, of course, but they stared at and thumbed their screens. A bite of a fresh waffle fry and a swipe on the phone. A sip on the straw of some sweet tea, and a click. These people had been sucked in like zombies to the smartphone "matrix." I couldn't help but shake my head as I realized even in the midst of connecting, they weren't. The real connection that could be happening around them had been replaced by a digital, lifeless transaction on their lit-up smartphones.

Bill and Angie had been coming to our Sunday night dinners for several weeks. We had known them for quite some time, and we thought they were connecting with our group. However, they didn't show up one week, and no one had heard from them. I reached out, but again, no response. After a few weeks of their absence, I knew something was way off. Again, our group tried to get in touch with them, and we began to pray more intentionally for them.

Finally, they came clean. In hindsight, it was obvious most of the communication we'd had from them up to that point hadn't been authentic or transparent. The reality was, their marriage was falling apart. Angie was moving out, and it was "he said, she said" anytime you spoke to one of them.

In an attempt to help save their marriage, a group of ladies met Angie for lunch at a nearby restaurant and asked questions while sharing love and consolation. Angie gave only vague answers and didn't seem interested in connecting. It was almost as if she didn't know *how* to connect.

The men made attempts to connect with Bill, who was more open. Angie and Bill at long last agreed to attend counseling sessions with a qualified third party. However, after a few months, this couple's inability to communicate—and continued isolation from each other—led to the end of their twenty-plus years of marriage.

James is a well-known public figure in the church world. He has written many books, spoken around the country, and taught at a Christian school. His messages and writings have been in high demand for many years. Countless young people and adults have gleaned much wisdom from his teachings.

James continuously poured into students, teaching them what it means to be a person of integrity and virtue. Many times, his secretary had to turn down opportunities for him to speak around the country because his calendar stayed so booked.

He was speaking at national events, representing his school and his church until . . . he disappeared. Not physically, obviously, but personally and ministry-wise, he dropped off the radar. He had been a dedicated family man, a serving person, and a popular speaker—but is now isolated because something happened. To date, no one knows what that "something" is, only that he left the school, canceled his speaking engagements, and vanished. While he was physically around hundreds of people every month, James was apparently alone, with no one to share his innermost struggles. Unfortunately, he didn't realize it didn't have to be that way.

Each of these stories are real even though the names have been changed. My heart aches at each one, and I wonder what could have gone differently. Why did this have to be the next step for each of these people? What would it have taken for the stories to have a different ending? What are the things that cause us to isolate ourselves?

You can find approaches to combat loneliness. All of them are, in my estimation, just ideas. Prepare yourself: some of them may shock you. Some of them may make you LOL (that's social media speak for laugh out loud, sorry).

Combating Loneliness Medically

Dr. Stephanie Cacioppo believes she might have an answer for loneliness. A prescription, a medicine—a pill that can soothe the brain activity that makes us feel such anguish when we are lonely. After her husband, John, died suddenly in his sleep at just sixty-six, Dr. Cacioppo, a professor of neuroscience and psychiatry at the University of Chicago, increased her determination in the war against loneliness.

Her most promising answer: pregnenolone, a steroid that our bodies make naturally. The Food and Drug Administration (FDA) considers it an acceptable (though not approved) supplement if it is an extract of the steroid—taken from an animal. But this steroid's ability to reduce the impact of stress on the body is being questioned.[1]

We try to medicate everything we can. While there may be some medicines that can help with loneliness, I personally would rather opt for some more practical ways to combat loneliness than an unapproved steroid derived from an animal. What will be next? A pill for humility? Pride? Anger?

Combating Loneliness through Chat Benches

Authorities in one small town are trying to make a difference in a more practical way. Police in the English seaside town of Burnham-on-Sea have installed "chat benches" to combat loneliness in the community.[2] A sign on the benches encourages someone feeling disconnected to have a seat and strike up a conversation with a "friendly stranger." Surprisingly, it's having a positive effect despite the fact that most of us grew up being told *not* to talk to strangers.

> "The Chat Bench is a very simple concept where a sign is placed on a bench, typically in a park or a town centre, in a location used

by a good cross-section of the community," said Burnham-on-Sea Police Community Support Officer (PCSO) Tracey Grobbeler. . . .

So far, two chat benches have been unveiled—one on the waterfront in the town and another next to a cafe in nearby Taunton. Each bench bears a welcoming sign for potential visitors: "The 'Happy to Chat' Bench: Sit Here If You Don't Mind Someone Stopping to Say Hello."

"The sign simply helps to break down the invisible, social barriers that exists between strangers who find themselves sharing a common place," said Grobbeler.

"Simply stopping to say 'hello' to someone at the Chat Bench could make a huge difference to the vulnerable people in our communities and help to make life a little better for them."[3]

The spokesperson said that not everyone has someone to talk to and that "many are suffering in silence without anyone to even ask how their day was."[4] People can make a big difference just by talking to someone.

How interesting! This town gets it. Conversation *does* make a difference. Communication with one another *is* part of the answer. Using our voices, inflections, facial expressions, and listening ears can all let people know that we care. I love this idea! I'm not sure chat benches would work in my city, but I'm excited this community is trying something creative. Let me share a couple more ideas.

In Austin, Texas, a nonprofit is fighting loneliness among the homeless in a very creative way. Their goal: to bring the most chronically homeless off the streets and give them a place to call home. "Providing a home," however, "is not enough," according to their founder, Alan Graham.

"We believe that housing will never solve homelessness, but community will," Graham told CNN.

"Because within each of us innately are two fundamental human desires *to be fully and wholly loved and to be fully and wholly known* and just stuffing somebody into a shelter or a house with four walls and a roof is nowhere near sufficient. It's all about the relationship here."[5]

What an interesting statement. Community and relationship are the answers, he says. And he's also spot-on when it comes to the fundamental human desires that are within each of us.

Another idea comes from Tony Dennis, a sixty-two-year-old security guard from London, who says his city is a city of "sociable loners."[6] Residents have very few ways to get to know one another. So, Tony joins some other friends in a monthly game that is hosted by the Cares Family, a charity aimed at curbing loneliness. Interestingly enough, the monthly gatherings intentionally mix *older people and young professionals* who are new to the area. The thirty-five-year-old founder, Alex Smith, believes that events like this will help people have a place to belong. They also connect two of the demographics that struggle most with loneliness: young professionals and the elderly.

This is a very interesting concept and one I believe communities across the United States should be trying. Not only would it help the two demographics that struggle with loneliness the most, but it would also help young professionals gain wisdom and knowledge from the older generation and perhaps be a real model for mentorship.

Combating Loneliness in College

Suicide is the tenth-leading cause of death across the US population but is the second-highest cause among college-aged students.[7] Many attribute this somber statistic to the issue of loneliness. The college years seem to be a very important time to combat the problem. The effects of loneliness are being felt on the campus of the University of Southern California, Los Angeles. Because of this, the Office of Religious Life has launched a new project called Campfires[8] aimed at connecting IRL (in real life), which encourages students to take time out from connecting with technology and to create and cultivate meaningful in-person relationships. There is specific training for advisors who are part of student life on campus to learn things such as how to cultivate intimacy in groups.

One of the best ways to cope with college loneliness is to recognize that it is a real threat to a new student who has moved away from family and friends and come to a brand-new environment with a brand-new schedule. Once the loneliness is recognized, proactive steps can be taken to keep it away.

I remember this feeling as a college student myself. I was in a new city with a new environment, new friends, new classes. There was very little that was familiar, and when things are unfamiliar, it's easy to get lonely because you have nothing you are used to. The best thing I chose to do was to get plugged in to a community group on campus.

For some students, getting involved in campus activities is a great way to overcome loneliness. But for some, that thought is overwhelming, especially when they are just getting used to a lot of other new things. Sometimes, the more active students are in outside activities, the better their academics will be. For shy or introverted students, getting involved or striking up conversations can seem like a daunting task and one they want to avoid at all costs. (We will talk more about some ways to develop friendships in the following chapter.)

Combating Loneliness through Technology

Some people are convinced we have to fight loneliness with technology. "Because technology can seemingly solve all our other problems?" I ask, tongue in cheek. In England, eighty-five-year-old Oslo, a widowed farmer,[9] admits he is lonely, despite the fact that his daughter lives nearby. He recently took part in a trial with a new device that inventors say looks like an old Etch A Sketch. On the device, pictures and messages that have been sent from his family rotate.

The same company that makes this device also has unveiled AV1, an AI (artificial intelligence) robot with cameras in its eye sockets. This robot allows people to feel present even if they aren't able to be somewhere in person. For example, children with chronic diseases who cannot attend school can feel as if they are present in class. AV1 is placed on a desk so absent children can follow along with what's going on in the room. "If they want to ask a question, they can press a button on the AV1 app and the top of the robot's head lights up."[10]

These "social robots" are being used in more places. One made by a Japanese company "can follow a person's gaze and model its behavior in response to humans."[11] Health care experts are already experimenting with robots in other ways, such as providing the elderly "bucket list" experiences so they won't have to leave their hospital beds. Welcome to the future. It's already here in the present.

Is this taking technology too far? Doesn't this push back into digital, lifeless connections? I'm not sure, but to me, it falls short of what my soul longs for.

Combating Loneliness through Renting Humans?

Technology may be able to solve the problem of loneliness in the future, but until then, other agencies have cropped up to offer real human contact to lonely people. Some agencies allow you to rent a family or friend to serve as a funeral mourner or simply be a companion for conversation. One such company in America will call and check on older relatives for a small monthly fee. Some organizations like this coordinate five hundred thousand calls a year where volunteers spend time talking to older people on the phone and carry on a conversation for fifteen minutes or so.[12] My friend's grandmother used to do this for free with telemarketers who interrupted her dinner. She would keep them on the phone for hours!

Another business that thinks there is no substitute for actual company (a real person) will connect younger people with older individuals who have a spare room for rent. The older person gets a roommate (for a discount on the rent), and it also solves the issue of loneliness. Users can sign up at an online portal and list their location and details on the room while would-be room seekers can go online and find a match in their preferred location. Some "nursing homes or local authorities are offering students free or cheap rent in exchange for helping out with housework."[13] Many start-ups like this really do want to disrupt loneliness and are trying to think outside the box when it comes to helping. What a great concept to connect two of the loneliest groups on the planet: the elderly and college students.

These ideas are all attempts to combat the issue of loneliness, but ultimately, are they accomplishing the goal? And even if they are helping, is there yet a better way of combating loneliness?

I believe so. I believe it comes down to relationships and community—but has culture itself set us up for failure when it comes to developing real relationships and authentic community?

We'll explore this in the next chapter.

PRACTICAL QUESTIONS TO CONSIDER

1. How do you see our world trying to combat loneliness? Are any of the ways working?

_____

_____

_____

2. How do you strive to overcome loneliness? Do any of these ways work? If so, why do you think they do? If not, why do you think they fall short?

_____

_____

_____

3. What do you believe is the primary obstacle to combating loneliness?

_____

_____

_____

PUT IT INTO PRACTICE

This is probably only for the brave at heart, but if you want to see how many are dealing with the issue of loneliness, try your own version of the "chat bench." You can go to a nearby park and make a sign on poster board that reads, "Free Conversations." If you aren't that brave, go to a nearby coffee shop, order two coffees, and sit down with someone who is alone to strike up a conversation. Give them the extra coffee, of course.

CHAPTER FOUR

Breaking the Pull of Isolation and Insulation

I have 2,775 friends. Facebook says so.

Anonymous

It was the middle of November, and I knew I had to do something. Running through the airports left me huffing and puffing, losing my breath, tired and weary—I needed to get back into shape. For the last year I had been working out two to three days a week, but something was missing. I wasn't sure what, but I was ready to find out. Although I'd asked for advice from friends on occasion, I hadn't gotten any real *inspiration*.

As I drove to the gym, I thought about how nice it would be to have someone to go with me. I lifted weights for about thirty minutes, then walked over to get on the treadmill when a guy dressed in trainer's attire walked over next to me. "Hey, man! I see you in here a lot. We haven't met. I work here. My name is Mike."

He extended his hand and I shook it. "Hey, Mike, I'm Jack."

"What are you trying to do with your workouts?" he asked. "I mean, what results do you want to see?"

I told Mike I'd like to lose a few pounds, tone up a bit, and get healthier. I wondered what his plan was. I was a little skeptical considering the plethora of "diet solutions" funneling through my social media feed every day.

Mike offered to meet with me three to four times a week if I wanted to text him when I was in town or headed to the gym. I figured I would give it a shot, and the next week I texted him. He gave me a suggested time to meet, and I put it on my calendar. The next day I walked into the gym in time for our 7:00 a.m. workout.

"Let's just take you through a basic workout, so I can see where you are," Mike said with a smile.

This former university football player looked at me as if he had found a fresh opponent to drag across the field, so needless to say, I was a little nervous. Sixty minutes later, after a few trips to the water fountain and with me dripping with sweat, we sat down in his office. I wasn't sure I would be able to stand back up.

"You did pretty good," he said with a smile. "I'd love to meet with you again if you want some help with your goals."

Little did I know what was in store as I nodded and began to plot dates on the calendar for more torture sessions. At least, that's what I called them that day. But six weeks later I was down twenty pounds, was stronger, and felt better than I had in a long time. That's the power of accountability and doing life with someone else. (And working with someone who knows the science of getting into shape.) And that's what happens when you get honest with someone else.

Honesty on the Beach

I remember another time I got honest. I was probably in my mid-twenties, leading a group event in Panama City, Florida. I had some good friends who had pointed me in the right direction, but I felt like my life was stagnant and I wasn't growing like I wanted. I had a great relationship with the friend who was leading the event with me. I trusted him and knew he loved me unconditionally, so I chose to be vulnerable and ask for his help. I decided that summer to open up every door of my heart, and I needed someone in whom I could confide, someone who would encourage me in my next steps.

I shared some of the struggles I was facing, the things that seemed to continue to ensnare me and my desire to live with integrity. It was an amazing conversation, because my friend shared some of the same struggles and challenges. That day we decided to engage in the kind of relationship I believe changed the trajectory of my life. Honesty with him, just like honesty with Mike at the gym, fueled the change I desired to see.

Two tendencies keep us from meaningful relationships: isolation and insulation. These two stories illustrate two powerful antidotes: accountability and authenticity.

Accountability Frees You from Isolation

There is no accountability without relationship. Accountability, however, is not synonymous with "relationship." Here's how accountability works. When I told Mike what I hoped to get from my workouts, accountability kicked in. It began because he approached me as a friend. He reminded me that he wanted the best for me. He committed to walk the road with me. We scheduled workouts, and it became harder to skip going to the gym because I knew Mike was waiting on me. Accountability pulls us out of isolation and into growing. If it's true for physical goals, it's also a principle that works in other areas of our lives.

Every January, without fail, workout facilities across the country are packed because of New Year's resolutions made by people who say they want to get into shape. After gorging ourselves during the holidays, we submit (at least for the short term) to rigid workouts to get in better physical shape. Most of our New Year's resolutions fail because most of us attempt them *all by ourselves.*

Accountability helps us stay healthy. Accountability fuels the discipline required to make us into mature people. And accountability will help us succeed.

Accountability is about both to WHAT and to WHOM you are accountable. Getting in shape is a good thing for which we need to be accountable, but perhaps the most powerful component of accountability is to whom we are accountable. Being accountable means living with integrity and following through on our commitments. It's about finding a way to show up and be present without expecting a certain outcome. It's living free from isolation and insulation, two things that can make us lonely.

Authenticity Frees You from Insulation

Insulation can be a good thing. The insulation in our homes helps keep the heat inside and the cold outside during the wintertime. That's a good use of insulation. But when we try to live our lives by ourselves, we insulate ourselves in a damaging way. Why?

Because it's impossible to be authentic by yourself. Being authentic implies a transparent connection with someone else.

Years ago, I used to travel around the country with a band and play music. The motley crew of guys would pack our gear into a van and trailer and set out for the next gig. Over the years, our equipment grew. We would pull up at an event and unload our sound board, speakers, lights, projectors and screens, fog machines, and the list goes on. Our band desired to put on a good show, do things professionally, and create an atmosphere for engagement.

48

When the event organizer introduced us, we came out on stage with lights flashing and fog in the air, and the crowd would start yelling and clapping. It was a great reception.

When the concert was over, people came to our merchandise table to buy our band T-shirts, CDs, and pictures. Many of them would ask for autographs, thinking we were important and famous. We weren't. We toured nationally, but we weren't famous. You haven't heard of us, have you?

For some reason or another, I never got that kind of reception at home. My wife and kids never asked for my autograph. And there was no applause or yelling when I got home. (They did run out to greet me with hugs and kisses depending on how long I had been on the road!)

My family knew the real me. The people who showed up at our concerts knew the guys they saw on stage, but not the real us. One of the greatest compliments I can receive is that I am *real*. When someone says that about me, I know my authenticity has been experienced by interacting and doing life with others. Those interactions have pruned me, or taken off the rough edges, and made me the real person I have become.

But how do we form real friendships? Adults in America certainly find it challenging. Barna research shows "the majority of adults has anywhere between two and five close friends (62%), but one in five regularly or often feels lonely." Our teens find it easier to connect—especially with differing groups: "Gen Z is the most diverse generation we've observed in American history, and this could be driving their engagement with those unlike them." That may make it easier for them to find acquaintances, but both groups still need to understand how to form real friendships."[1]

Friendships are challenging because there's no legal bond like in a marriage. There's paperwork that makes the marriage official, right? And there's no blood connection in a friendship like in family relationships. "We choose our friends, and our friends choose us," says William K. Rawlins, Stocker Professor of Communication Studies at Ohio University. "That's a really distinctive attribute of friendships."[2]

Jeffrey Hall, an associate professor of communication studies at the University of Kansas, recently conducted a study in which he determined it takes about fifty hours of time together for two people to become "casual friends" and at least two hundred hours of quality time to become close friends.[3] Whether you believe the statistics, the reality is that it does **take time** to build close friendships, and few of us seem to be willing to make that investment these days.

A Creative Way to Make a Difference and Make Friends

I was twenty years old, summer break was over, and I was about to head back to college. Before the summer break, the relationship with my only real college girlfriend had ended. I was lonely and probably a little depressed. The fall semester started, and I tried to get back into a routine, but I found it difficult. The month of September chugged along until a weather report rolled in that caught everyone's attention.

You see, as the fall months approach, the weather patterns off the coast of the southeastern United States lend themselves to hurricanes. The fall of 1989 was no different. In fact, the impending Hurricane Hugo was headed up the Carolina coastline and would wind up bringing major devastation.

At the time, it was ranked as the costliest hurricane to hit the U.S. mainland, with damages totaling $7 billion (1989 USD/$13.43 billion 2014 USD), until Andrew in 1992.

Hugo made landfall over Sullivan's Island, South Carolina, about midnight EDT on September 22, 1989. Hugo was a Category 4 hurricane at landfall with winds of about 140 mph.[4]

I was at school at Gardner-Webb College (now a university) in Boiling Springs, North Carolina, just outside of Shelby and close to Charlotte. When Hugo hit, we felt the effects all the way up to Boiling Springs, and even in the city of Charlotte, more than two hundred miles from the coastline. I remember the trash can outside my apartment was blown across the field near my home. It was a devastating hurricane that left a lasting impression.

As we received word of the destruction, many college students mobilized to do something. I joined a group of students headed to the South Carolina coast with a few supplies, a couple pairs of gloves, and determination to help. The impact I saw was unlike anything I'd seen before.

I felt like I was driving into a movie set when I spotted the huge yachts sitting on houses miles from the shoreline. What was amazing was that many of the yachts had no damage whatsoever. It was as if a giant hand had picked them up and moved them inland dozens of miles. Before our arrival, connections had been made for us through one of our contacts, and when we climbed out of our vehicles, we were assigned a section off the shoreline to help clean up. They were not letting just anyone into this area for safety and security reasons. Our task was to throw debris into large dump trucks that were lined up by the dozens to carry the glass, lumber, fallen trees, pieces of houses, etc., to another location.

After an hour or so of working full throttle, I began talking with the students and other people who had shown up to help. We were united in the cleanup effort. I met people from all over the East Coast who had come to help. Even though dump truck after dump truck kept rolling away with debris, it didn't look like we were making much progress, but we kept working.

"Hey, this truck needs to get moving!" someone yelled.

"Can you drive it?" someone else shouted, looking at me.

I hesitated, not sure how to answer. Yes, I knew how to drive, but . . .

"Jump in this truck and follow the one in front of you. We've got to keep these trucks moving," the guy said, pushing me toward the driver's door.

I looked at him with an "are you sure?" look and he said, "Get going!"

The next thing I knew, I was driving a dump truck down Highway 17 in a caravan of others. I wasn't sure if I needed a special license or if it really mattered at this point. What an experience!

Volunteering

There's something to be said about volunteering. That experience moved me out of my loneliness because it took my attention off myself and my sorrow over the breakup. Looking back, I think I was unaware of how positive this distraction was for me.

In a recent survey of over ten thousand people in the UK, two-thirds reported that volunteering helped them feel less isolated. Similarly, a 2018 study of nearly six thousand people across the United States examined widows who, unsurprisingly, felt lonelier than married adults. After starting to volunteer for two or more hours per week, their feelings of loneliness seemed to ease up as well.[5]

Volunteering and serving are great ways to meet people with whom you share common values and bonds. And they help out someone else as well. This common cause, whether it be helping the elderly, serving in a soup kitchen, or working with a Big Brothers Big Sisters of America program, will connect you with others and allow you to make new friends. When we volunteer for causes that are important to us, we can find a renewed sense of purpose, which in turn makes us feel better and relieves the negative emotion of loneliness.

Connections

Whether it's volunteering, joining a club, or eating with a friend, connections are important. These friendships allow us to connect in authenticity with another person. They also give us someone with whom to share personal details of our life, so we can gain encouragement. Opening up and sharing and working together make a powerful difference.

Still need convincing? We'll look at some "together" moments in the next chapter.

PRACTICAL QUESTIONS TO CONSIDER

1. What do you think makes a good friendship? Name several people you would call good friends.

2. What kind of person does it take to have an accountable relationship?

3. Why do you think authenticity in relationships is so hard
to accomplish today? What can we do to build authenticity into our relationships?

_____

_____

_____

PUT IT INTO PRACTICE

I have two assignments for you.

One, begin thinking now about someone who loves you unconditionally who could serve you as an accountability partner,
someone who could help you grow and with whom you could have
an honest friendship.

Two, find somewhere to volunteer. It doesn't have to be many
hours a week, maybe it's just one. It could be at a daycare, the
library, your church, a school. Find somewhere that you can use
your gifts and talents and serve someone. Once you have signed
up, send me an email at jack@jackeason.com and let me know.

CHAPTER FIVE

Fitting in at Starbucks

Why are you trying so hard to fit in when you were
born to stand out?

Ian Wallace

I'm not a coffee drinker. I've tried to like it, but since I grew up in the South, sweet tea is my default. I'm not complaining. It's made me who I am. No, seriously, I think it's running through my veins.

On a spring break trip to New York City with my son, Will, I began to be aware of a growing community. We had headed out early one morning and were looking for a place to quickly grab some caffeine and start sightseeing. Since sweet tea was virtually nonexistent in New York City, we opted to dart into a Starbucks to have one made for me. The barista looked at me funny when I said "sweet" tea, but nonetheless, she obliged. After grabbing my tea and Will's hot chocolate, we headed back out into the cold to begin our early morning excursion. As we crossed one street and turned down another, I felt like we were walking in circles. I looked up and there it was . . . another Starbucks. I laughed out loud. It seemed like there was one on every corner, and that's probably close to being true. I looked it up. There are over 240 Starbucks in Manhattan alone.[1] *Unbelievable.*

That fact intrigues me because I do a lot of training for organizations around the country. I often use Starbucks as an example when it comes to marketing and branding. Whether you like their coffee or not, they're doing something right. In most Starbucks I've gone to, they have a lot of people inside, most of whom share a love for coffee. But if you do research on the company, they'll admit to you that the focus really isn't the coffee.

Inspiring and Nurturing

According to Starbucks's website, their mission is *"to inspire and nurture the human spirit—one person, one cup and one neighborhood at a time."*[2]

Pretty simple, right? Are they accomplishing this mission of nurturing and inspiring? It sure looks like it. The basic definitions of inspire and nurture are to "fill someone with the urge to feel something" and to "encourage." Are those the kind of community and relationships you're looking for? I think it's safe to say those are the kind of community and relationships we're all looking for. We want real relationships that will inspire and encourage us; none of us are looking for relationships that will depress us or discourage us. So, what can we learn from the Starbucks community? Is there more beyond the connections that might be taking place at Starbucks, and if so, what is it?

A Sense of Belonging

The need to belong is a human emotional need. We all desire to affiliate with and be accepted by members of a group. This may be a peer group at school, colleagues in our workplace, an athletic team, or a group of people with whom we share our faith. Every person searches for *a sense of belonging.*

The need to belong drives us to seek out these stable, long-lasting relationships with other people. Thankfully, we're born with this desire to connect with other people. It motivates us to participate in all kinds of organizations. Moving through life alone is *not* our only choice. When we are part of a group, we realize we can accomplish something bigger than we can by ourselves.

Fitting in and belonging are not the same thing. "*Fitting in . . .* is assessing situations and groups of people, then twisting yourself into a human pretzel in order to get them to let you hang out with them. *Belonging* is something else entirely—it's showing up and letting yourself be seen and known as you really are—love of gourd painting, intense fear of public speaking and all."[3]

Many of us suffer from this mental dichotomy of who we are and who we present to the world in order to be accepted, but it doesn't have to be that way. So, why do we try to pretend to be something or someone we're not? Where does that come from? Perhaps the pressure comes from our obsession with social media, where we make assumptions based on one picture posted from a person's day that makes it seem they're living in paradise—or at least the good life. Oh, that we could pick different "freeze frames" from that person's day and see the reality that doesn't show up on their news feed. Pretending to be something we are not isn't a healthy way to live.

People search for a place of belonging. A sense of security in being authentic and knowing they'll be accepted for who they are.

For a lot of us, according to Starbucks, this sense of belonging is found when gathering with other coffee drinkers.

Neutral Space, Equal Footing, Welcoming

Starbucks speaks often about a "third place" that is neither work nor home but rather a neutral *community* space, a space where people can meet on an *equal footing*.

Perhaps that's the basis for unity. Did you notice that *unity* is part of the word *community*? But what is unity? *Merriam-Webster's Dictionary* says it is "the quality or state of being one."[4]

Perhaps the secret to unity begins with how we view ourselves within the community **along with** how we view others.

I think Starbucks is on to something. The company realizes you may pay a little more for their coffee, but you're willing to do so because you're also getting a pleasant, inviting place where you can hang out, not to mention the bonus of free internet. This neutral, inviting space where everyone is equal is attractive to people. Why would it not be attractive? There are few places like this in the world; however, I've seen this kind of space in my own home.

A few weeks ago, my wife and I wrapped up a four-week couples' study in our home. It was probably one of the most enjoyable things we've done in a while. I think everyone who attended would agree. We put the word out on social media (yes, it can be used for good things) and waited to see who would respond. We didn't want a large group, because we wanted to get to know one another. After a few days, we had five couples, counting us. We didn't know two of the couples; one couple we vaguely knew, and the other couple were close friends.

Each week we picked a theme, brought a corresponding pot-luck food item, and gathered around our table to eat and talk about being married. We were a diverse group. A young couple in their twenties who'd been married for five years. Another couple who had thirty years under their belts. And Lynette and I laid claim to twenty-three years. There was also one soon-to-be-married couple brave enough to join us. They seemed to be the most excited about this fun experience. They wanted to learn from the "experts." We were diverse, but we were meeting in a "homey" environment, and all of us *felt* we were on equal footing.

In the midst of a lot of laughter, the soon-to-be newlyweds heard some of the comments from the "veterans." And there was even more laughter from the veterans at some of the naïve comments that came from the soon-to-be newlyweds. But we all discovered something very powerful during our time together. Those of us who had been married the longest were able to share insights with those who were just beginning to navigate the waters of married life. We were able to serve as a tangible GPS, if you will, for those looking for instructions and directions. It was *very* satisfying for everyone.

Here's something that hit home for me.

Like the engaged couple or the couple with five years of marriage, we all need people who have "been there" to show us the way. We need people in our lives who will walk with us, who will be willing to open their hearts so that we can learn from their mistakes as well as their wisdom. Likewise, some of the veterans needed to be reminded of that "falling in love" feeling they'd had at the beginning of their relationship and to remember the commitment they made at the start.

Our group showed us it's difficult to discover truth in a vacuum. We discovered truth as one person after another told their stories. As someone with more experience and wisdom shed light on an issue relating to marriage, eyes would brighten. We all reaped the benefits because we met each other on **equal ground.**

Consistency

I've noticed something else at Starbucks: *you always know what you are getting*. It's the same burnt-coffee smell, same jazz music, same leather furniture and wood-grained ambiance. The hum and spray of the espresso machines is a predictable sound in each store. And the corporate bigwigs at Starbucks would tell you that each of those things is intentional. You know what to expect. I've been in Starbucks all over the world, and it's always the same. I always know what I'm getting.

People like consistency. While we find it at Starbucks and other chain stores, consistency is rare in our relationships. Finding people who are consistent and act with integrity is a challenge. You may find someone who models genuine behavior one day, and then the next day they are far from it in a confusing case of Dr. Jekyll, Mr. Hyde.

I'm not suggesting any of us are without fault or we will never let people down. I let people down more often than I'd like. However, the point I'm making is that consistency is a big deal. If I try a restaurant one day and the service and food are great, but the next week the service is horrendous and the food is cold, I won't be going back to that place. The same with a community. If you don't have a consistent experience, you likely won't go back. The current generation not only would *not* go back but would leave a bad review on Yelp or some other social media network. We are looking for those kinds of people and places that show consistency.

Are We Consistent?

When you hang out with people on a regular basis, they get to know the "real you." And if they love you enough, they will be honest and forthright when they believe you are getting off track.

Have you ever traveled with someone who you thought you knew but really didn't? In 2014 three of my friends and I traveled to Malawi, Africa, to train pastors. On our first visit, we knew little about the mission and little about where we would be staying. We didn't know what we would be eating. To be honest, we didn't know much about the whole trip, other than we felt like we were supposed to go and serve the people there.

Our flight from the United States to Johannesburg, South Africa, was seventeen hours. When you spend seventeen hours on a plane with someone, you learn a thing or two. I learned which movies my friends liked and also that one of them was a peanut addict, since every time the flight attendant passed by, he asked for another pack of peanuts. After watching two movies and taking a short nap, I thought we were getting close to landing. When I asked the flight attendant how close we were to Africa, she smiled and said, "Sir, we aren't even halfway yet."

In Johannesburg, we spent the night and then flew out the next day to Malawi. When we finally arrived in Malawi, we were exhausted. All we wanted was a gallon of ice-cold water to drink and a long, hot shower. After meeting the team at the airport and shaking hands, we piled into the car and headed toward our accommodations. Needless to say, it wasn't a four-star hotel. I'm not even sure it would have garnered one star. There was no air-conditioning, only occasional electricity, and every once in a while, there was water. I remember midway through our week coming back to the "lodge" to try to take a shower and standing under the drip-drip-drip lathered up with soap only to have the water stop completely. It was quite the experience.

I mean that sincerely. I wouldn't trade it for anything. During that trip, I saw the *consistency* of my three friends. They all had the attitude of servants. They never missed a beat. Were we challenged with our accommodations? Absolutely. Was it difficult? Most definitely. Did we want to come home a few times? Yep. But the consistency I saw in the lives of these three friends made me respect them more. And together we pushed through, did what we came to do, and went home fulfilled. You know what I realized during that time? Another word for consistency might be *integrity*. Integrity is "an unimpaired condition."[5]

Integrity is living a consistent life. Without integrity, there is no unity. And integrity is the foundation for trust. Which is inspiring.

Are We Inspiring?

Is inspiration missing in our relationships? Inspiration causes us to rise above our ordinary experiences to new heights. It propels us to see and do things we never felt would be possible. It even helps us to go beyond what we think we can accomplish.

Psychologists Todd M. Thrash and Andrew J. Elliot developed the "Inspiration Scale," which measures how much inspiration a person experiences each day. They discovered

> that inspired people were more open to new experiences and re-ported more absorption in their tasks. . . . Inspired individuals also reported having a stronger drive to master their work but were less competitive, which makes sense if you think of competition as a non-transcendent desire to outperform competitors. Inspired people were more intrinsically motivated and less extrinsically mo-tivated, variables that also strongly impact work performance. . . . Inspired people also reported higher levels of important psycholog-ical resources, including belief in their own abilities, self-esteem, and optimism. Mastery of work, absorption, creativity, perceived competence, self-esteem, and optimism were all consequences of inspiration, suggesting that inspiration facilitates these important psychological resources.[6]

Sounds like inspiration is an important thing.

Inspiration is not the same as just creating a positive effect.

Compared to being in an enthusiastic and excited state, people who enter an inspired state (by thinking of a prior moment they were inspired) reported greater levels of spirituality and meaning, and lower levels of volitional control, controllability, and self-responsibility for their inspiration. Whereas positive affect is activated when someone is making progress toward their immediate, conscious goals, inspiration is more related to an awakening to something new, better, or more important: transcendence of one's previous concerns.[7]

We need the kinds of relationships and community that will be consistent and inspire us to do greater things together. Starbucks may seem like it gets it, but there are those who believe Starbucks has built its company on the "loneliness of American consumers, and their desire to be lonely in company."[8] It's interesting to see that many times in the crowded spaces of Starbucks, there are individuals working on laptops, sipping coffee, but still **all alone**. The money Starbucks makes selling togetherness is amazing, but is what Starbucks is offering enough?

PRACTICAL QUESTIONS TO CONSIDER

1. Who exemplifies inspiration and nurturing to you? What is it about the person that makes you think of them? What can you learn from them?

2. What are the traits you think are important in community?

_____

_____

_____

3. How important is consistency and inspiration when finding community?

_____

_____

_____

4. Where do you receive that sense of belonging and inspiration?

_____

_____

_____

PUT IT INTO PRACTICE

Take about forty-five minutes out of your week to sit down and find a show called *Cheers*. You can probably find it with a streaming service or on YouTube. As you watch an episode, make some notes about what you see that builds a sense of belonging. How are people connecting? Are they feeling inspired? What things seem to be helping build community?

CHAPTER SIX

An Imperfect Group of People

Have no fear of perfection—you'll never reach it.

Salvador Dali

I was sitting at home, channel surfing to take a mental break, and I landed on a new show from Ellen DeGeneres. I will admit it. I'm an Ellen fan. While we may disagree on some issues, I find her compassion and genuine love for people to be something I would love to emulate in my own life. She's imperfect—just like me. On this particular show, she'd gathered a group of people to receive some gifts from her, but they thought they had come together to see a premiere of a play she was in. When she walked out onstage to welcome them to the play, she told them that was not why they were invited. Instead, she shared that they were going to be part of a great gift giveaway.

Great Gift Giveaway

One of the families Ellen decided to help was a family of three: a dad and two daughters. One of the daughters had sent a video to Ellen asking for her help. The girls' mom had passed away, and the family was finding it difficult to move forward and this young girl was lonely. The dad was doing his best to raise two teenage daughters, and graduation for them both was approaching. Ellen called the family out of the audience to sit on the stage with her and share their story with the crowd. After a few questions, Ellen said she had a gift for the family, and they were given a small replica of the Eiffel Tower.

"I know from what you have shared that your mom loved the Eiffel Tower, right?" she asked them.

"Yes, she did, and she had always hoped that we would one day go as a family," one of the daughters answered.

"Well, that's wonderful, so that replica can remind you of her dream—but better yet, I think I will just send you and your family to Paris!" Ellen said with excitement.

Cue confetti. Fire the music. Audience screams. And, of course, the tears. I may or may not have needed a Kleenex. Ellen went on to share that since they would be so close to Italy, Greece, and London, they might as well see those places too.[1]

It's not just a story about making people's dreams come true. I think Ellen genuinely wants people to know she cares. She wants them to know they are not alone. And she is using her platform and resources to meet the needs of others and give them a sense of belonging. Do you think this resonates with people? Considering her talk show is over seventeen years old and has spawned other shows, I would say yes!

Ellen's idea of helping people belong and meeting needs is a wonderful example of one person trying to build community and aid people dealing with loneliness, but have you ever seen this demonstrated in a group?

Facebook Christmas Heroes

I'm not sure if you have seen the commercial. A young woman serving in the army is sitting at a computer screen, posting on Facebook. She is part of a young mothers' group, and she posts that she's away on military assignment and is sorrowful about not being able to be home for Christmas.

The Facebook group springs into action, going shopping for her husband and kids, getting a Christmas tree, and even sneaking in and decorating the young woman's home. Much to her family's surprise, they come home one evening to find the gifts, the lights, and the home fully decorated. Then the camera switches to an outside shot, where we see one of the partygoers left on the roof, shaking a box of fake snow over the edge. As the fake snow falls in front of the living room window, the kids exclaim, "It's snowing!" The last shot is the young military mother video-calling her family and seeing the results of her "group heroes" making her Christmas wish come true. It's a great commercial about doing life together. It's exactly what we are talking about as one of the best solutions to loneliness.

The Power of a Faith Community

God created us with this longing inside for community. It's by design. We were not meant to live alone or be disconnected. In fact, community is one of the strong evidences for the existence of God.

Jesus said in John 17:21–23,

> The goal is for all of them to become one heart and
>   mind—
> Just as you, Father, are in me and I in you,

So they might be one heart and mind with us.
Then the world might believe that you, in fact, sent me.
The same glory you gave me, I gave them,
So they'll be united and together as we are—
I in them and you in me.
Then they'll be mature in this oneness,
And give the godless world evidence
That you've sent me and loved them
In the same way you've loved me. (Message)

As powerful as one person can be to help defeat the feelings of loneliness, a group of people is even more powerful. And as powerful as a group can be, I'm convinced a group that has a common faith can be even more powerful. Despite its problems and challenges, the church can be and should be a monumental force in helping connect people and overcome the issue of loneliness.

Perhaps you have tried a faith community and found yourself let down. I understand. You're not alone. Welcome to the real world. As long as we're trying to connect with other people, we will find disappointment and discouragement along the way. But we can't give up.

It dumbfounds me when I hear people make comments like, "I've tried church and didn't find real community there." Usually those comments come with some ideal standard in the person's mind to which they're comparing a church they left. Perhaps the ideal that they have in their mind is an obstacle to real community.

We would never view other relationships the way we sometimes talk about church. For example, I would have never married the most phenomenal woman in the world if I had given up after going out with only one young lady.

"I've tried dating and I didn't find the woman I was looking for, so I am giving it up."

"I tried eating out, but that restaurant didn't serve me well, so I'm not going to eat anymore."

That kind of thinking would be ludicrous, wouldn't it? The German pastor Dietrich Bonhoeffer apparently couldn't understand statements like these either. He suggested our ideals sometimes don't equate to reality: "Every human wish dream that is injected into the Christian community is a hindrance to genuine community and must be banished if genuine community is to survive. He who loves his dream of a community more than the Christian community itself becomes a destroyer of the latter, even though his personal intentions may be ever so honest and earnest and sacrificial."[2] Could it be that the community of our imagination is an enemy of the actual community to which we are to belong?

Casey McCall says it this way:

> Dreams are always abstractions. When we imagine the ideal Christian community in the abstract, we eliminate any possibility of loving and being loved. Follow me here: If I enter into a particular community, expecting that community to fulfill my dream of what a community should be, then people become abstract props in my dream. I am not serving them. I am not committed to them. I do not love them. I am expecting them to play their parts in my dream. If they fail to meet my expectations, I drop them and continue my search for the dream community—one that I will never find. The language being used may sound spiritually mature as the seeker expresses criticisms over lack of "love" and "fellowship," but the only hindrance to said love and fellowship is the dreamer.[3]

Let's face it. You and I both are imperfect. But, as imperfect as we are, we can find community and leave loneliness behind if we are willing to look for it. And looking for it requires investing and committing.

Investing and Committing

If you are going to ever find real community and connection, you have to be willing to invest. Investing means showing up, being present, and having a willingness to have relationships where you are not only receiving something but willing to give something. When I make a financial investment, I let go of some of my money and relinquish it to someone else. That "letting go" is a critical part of being able to discover connectedness. And, yes, it's scary, but it is part of the journey of finding friendship and community. What makes it easier within a faith community is that you share the common bond of belief in Jesus. That is the foundational part of the relationship.

The second part that is critical to finding connection in the church is committing. I remember visiting many churches over the years. A few years ago, my wife and I moved to a new city and visited twenty to twenty-five churches, looking for connectivity. I remember sitting in a service and saying to my wife, "I wish we could find somewhere that feels like home." Her response was, "Maybe if we stayed here a while?" Sound advice. "To feel at home in a place, you have to have some prospect of staying there."[4] You have to commit yourself to the people of that fellowship.

She was right. If you enter into a community (or any relationship) with unrealistic expectations, half-heartedness, and hesitancy, you will never find a place that feels like home. If you and I want to find a place to belong, we have to commit. We can't try to be connected and at the same time remain a step away. It's awkward for us and the community of which we are a part.

I wanted the feeling and atmosphere of the last church we attended. But that wasn't fair to this new faith community. They were not the same people. The church was not the same church. And the reality is, no two churches are the same. I can't expect my experiences of one church to match those of another church. Embracing this new community with an excitement for its possibilities gives me the opportunity to have connectedness with this group of people. After all, the goal in community with others is love.

> By this all people will know that you are my disciples, if you have love for one another. (John 13:35 ESV)

Are you ready to consider the church as a prime place to build community? I hope so, because the benefits far exceed simply overcoming loneliness. And the benefits come from doing life . . . together.

PRACTICAL QUESTIONS TO CONSIDER

1. If you are part of a faith community, take a moment and write down some of the ways you are investing in that community. Think about how others are investing as well.

2. What other examples can you think of in which one individual is doing something to combat loneliness? What are some things groups are doing to help overcome loneliness?

3. Is there anything the faith community is doing in your
   area to provide a solution for loneliness?

   _____

   _____

   _____

PUT IT INTO PRACTICE

If you have invested and committed to a faith community, get together with some in your community and talk about how God is connecting you despite your imperfections.

If you are not a part of a faith community consistently, take a few weeks and visit some churches in your area with an open mind. After each visit, take a moment to write down the positive things you saw happening in that community despite imperfect people.

PART TWO

The Loneliness Solution

CHAPTER SEVEN

The Power of WE

Alone we can do so little; *together* we can do so much.

Helen Keller

As the nation watched on TV, three heroic astronauts made an amazing journey toward the moon. Some people said it could never be done. Yet on July 16, 1969, three astronauts took off into space, and eventually, two stepped onto the moon's surface, creating history. They became the first human beings to set foot onto another planetary body. People around the nation watched on TV and cheered at this phenomenal accomplishment. If you were alive during this event, you will never forget it as long as you live.

While Neil Armstrong, Buzz Aldrin, and Michael Collins are the well-known faces of this fantastic achievement, they wouldn't have made it into the history books without the efforts of a huge supporting team—years of research and expertise allowed this mission to succeed.

For over twenty-four months prior to the operation, mission planners studied the moon's surface ad nauseam. They used photographs from satellites and other spacecraft to find the best place for Apollo 11 to land. The planners and scientists, along with engineers, needed to consider the geography of the surface of the moon, factoring in craters, boulders, and cliffs, as well as the timing for the spacecraft to land, keeping in mind the position of the sun.

NASA has estimated that *more than four hundred thousand people* made the historic moon landing possible.[1] There were scientists, engineers, and technicians who had never worked in aerospace before. These people were given contracts to design a machine capable of transporting humans safely to outer space. Sounds like some scary responsibility to me.

The technicians visited the laboratories to create a human connection with the space travelers so they would be unified as a team. It was important for the workers to meet the men whose lives would be in their hands. In the operations control room, during each flight, there were numerous technicians guiding and supporting those heading into space. Each step of the way, in every part of the process, honest communication with one another enabled the team behind NASA's Apollo 11 to achieve a historic milestone. We are better *together. The Apollo landing has impacted all of human history.*

Nature holds examples of being *better together.* Every winter flocks of geese work together to achieve their common goal—*reaching their destination.* Communicating by honking at one another, they encourage each other along the way in case one should lose momentum or get tired. Collectively, they push forward, focused on the mission of arriving safely at the next stop on the journey.

By flying in a V-shape formation, the geese reduce the drag for those behind them. The lead goose points the way and keeps the destination in mind. These same principles could be implemented among groups today. By nurturing this team mentality, all members of the flock share a common goal and feel supported by one another because they are working *together*.

These stories from technology and nature are only two of a plethora of examples where we see that we are better together. We don't talk about this much in our society. Most of the time we work as competitors, and we're trained that way from the beginning. Whether it's in sports, education, or, most certainly, the workplace, the mindset is to be number one. If one wants to be considered successful, one must earn that title. Top dog versus underdog. First versus second. Winner versus loser.

A common mindset is that if someone else gets more, we get less. It's the "look out for number one" mentality that runs rampant in our culture. The fact that we could accomplish something or be better by joining forces with someone else is all too often a foreign concept.

Todd Davis calls this the "win-lose" mindset.[2] He states this weakens the trust of others and ultimately decreases productivity in the work environment. *I* would add it weakens productivity in every environment. Could it be God gives us different strengths so we would *have* to work?

Davis describes another attitude called the "lose-win" mindset.[3] This is the belief that if someone else wins, I have to give up, because there's no worth in trying anymore. This creates bitterness and isolation. We sure see this in our political landscape, don't we?

Neither of these mindsets is healthy.

I've come to believe that the best mindset is the "win-win" one. This requires "thinking *we*, not *me*." Kind of hard to do, isn't it? Davis says it requires two essential elements: courage and consideration. "Courage," he says, "is the willingness . . . to speak your thoughts respectfully." Consideration is the willingness to let others do the same.[4]

I don't know about you, but I'm seeing a whole lot of "courage" on social media, and not a lot of consideration. People want to express their thoughts and be heard respectfully, but when it's time for the other person to do the same, the willingness goes out the window. That's not a good formula for building relationships, let alone any kind of meaningful friendship.

So, let's think about this. How can we practically show courage and consideration in our relationships? How can we "think we, not me"?

Davis makes a few suggestions:

- Wait to speak until several others have shared their ideas.
- Ask for input before sharing your thoughts.
- Turn off all devices and make eye contact when talking with people.
- Don't interrupt.
- Try going with someone else's decision (in a low-risk situation first) to see how it affects the relationship.[5]

If we engaged people with this level of courage and consideration, can you imagine how our conversations and relationships might change? If this togetherness can make such a difference in nature and in humans in our earthly pursuits, **can you imagine the impact we could have working together to accomplish the things God has called us to do?**

Have you thought about applying these same concepts to your faith? Have you thought about the spiritual benefits of what we could accomplish for God's kingdom by doing things together? Maybe you're wondering if that kind of consideration and courage can exist within a group of people. I assure you, it can.

Let me share an example.

"Not Me, but We" Works

Most people live compartmentalized lives. We work over here, we put family over there, and our faith is in another box altogether. However, if we could see life through the lens of faith, all of our endeavors could be opportunities to express God's goodness throughout the earth. What happens when a group of individuals not only believes this to be true but utilizes their combined faith to work together to demonstrate the love of Christ? There is always a ripple effect that changes innumerable lives.

But it takes *courage and consideration.*

In a small, quaint town in Florida, many people live in poverty. Drugs are easily accessible and much of the population lacks health insurance. Bob is an alcoholic who received help at the local men's center. Sierra is a precious eleven-year-old girl, abused and abandoned by her parents, who is now at a nearby children's shelter, safe from harm. An elderly man named Doug, who has been diagnosed with several ailments, was cared for at a clinic. Each of these people—Bob, Sierra, and Doug—received wonderful care and concern because of a group of people in Leesburg, Florida, who understand *we are better together.* In each of these circumstances, Leesburg people have succeeded in mending broken lives and serving the public good. Their success is no accident.

This group is part of the faith community at First Baptist Church, Leesburg, and has made it their mission to accept a deep, personal responsibility and love for those in need. This responsibility is grounded in an abiding *sense of belonging and friendship* they have with their community (remember this sense of belonging, we will talk more about it later) and their faith that touches every area in the lives of people they have community with.

This "better-togetherness" enabled this group to open a rescue mission in 1982. Shortly thereafter, they created a separate facility for abused children. And in 1987, the believers realized many in their community were dealing with unplanned pregnancies, so they opened a center to serve those ladies. And two years later, they opened a home for displaced women and children, victims of domestic abuse. Taking notice of the needs in their community gave them a vision to operate a ministry village that now consists of seven facilities on four acres of land operated by over five hundred volunteers from the church's ministry.[6]

The strong relational bond they have among the people they serve comes from spending time with them as they have discovered the needs of families and children alike. These volunteers "are motivated by the sense of belonging that they experience as a part of the church" family.[7] What a great motivation! Isn't it also interesting what can be accomplished when you're not concerned about who gets the credit? (Or in this case, they wanted God to get the credit.)

Their pastor emeritus, Charles Roesel, who retired in 2006 after serving the church for thirty years, explains this sense of belonging with the Greek term *koinonia*:

> "*Koinonia* is a deep sense of belonging to one another," which sustains people in the challenging and difficult work of serving the neediest. "If God's people are to witness and minister to a lost and hurting world," states Roesel, "*koinonia* must be the sustaining context in which they find their strength and will to do so."[8]

Was it easy for the group of believers to get to this place? Not really. In the early 1980s, when someone spoke up about starting this ministry to the citizens of Leesburg, the members of the church originally refused the idea:

Roesel says his congregation struggled with the same concerns that likely prevent other congregations from taking similar actions in their communities. Some FBC members were afraid that the new ministry would attract unfamiliar and indigent people into their midst [people who were not really like them]. Others were concerned about focusing too narrowly on social action, a concern propelled by the social gospel movement of the early 1900s.[9]

This movement thought the church should take care of everybody's needs and wasn't concerned a lot with people coming to know Christ. The reality is, there needs to be a balanced approach, as First Baptist discovered. Eventually, the desire to meet needs in their community overpowered any discomfort or angst they felt about moving forward.

People don't care how much you know until they know how much you care. It might be cliché, but it's true.

FBC's ministries succeeded in part because they refused to narrow the focus of their faith. They decided to take social action that is integrated with the core tenets of their members' faith. They also decided that if they worked together, they could accomplish something no one person—no matter how talented or passionate—could do alone. And they discovered they were right. That is the difference one group can make when they decide to do something **together**.

Together Is the Answer

The Scriptures are full of the idea of togetherness. Scripture often uses the phrase "one another." We read about loving one another, bearing one another's burdens, praying for one another.

"One another" is two words in English, but it's only one word in Greek. It's used one hundred times in ninety-four New Testament verses. Forty-seven of those verses give instructions to the church, and 60 percent of those instructions come from Paul.

When you look at these verses, a few more common themes show up:

Unity. One-third of the "one another" commands deal with the unity of the church.

1. Be at peace with one another (Mark 9:50).
2. Don't grumble among one another (John 6:43).
3. Be of the same mind with one another (Rom. 12:16; 15:5).
4. Accept one another (Rom. 15:7).
5. Wait for one another before beginning the Eucharist (1 Cor. 11:33).
6. Don't bite, devour, and consume one another (Gal. 5:15).
7. Don't boastfully challenge or envy one another (Gal. 5:26).
8. Gently, patiently tolerate one another (Eph. 4:2).
9. Be kind, tenderhearted, and forgiving to one another (Eph. 4:32).
10. Bear with and forgive one another (Col. 3:13).
11. Seek good for one another, and don't repay evil for evil (1 Thess. 5:15).
12. Don't complain against one another (James 4:11; 5:9).
13. Confess sins to one another (James 5:16).

Love. One-third of them instruct Christians to love one another.

1. Love one another (John 13:34; 15:12, 17; Rom. 13:8; 1 Thess. 3:12; 4:9; 1 Pet. 1:22; 1 John 3:11; 4:7, 11; 2 John 5).
2. Through love, serve one another (Gal. 5:13).
3. Tolerate one another in love (Eph. 4:2).

4. Greet one another with a kiss of love (1 Pet. 5:14).

5. Be devoted to one another in love (Rom. 12:10).

Humility. About 15 percent stress an attitude of humility and deference among believers.

1. Give preference to one another in honor (Rom. 12:10).

2. Regard one another as more important than yourselves (Phil. 2:3).

3. Serve one another (Gal. 5:13).

4. Wash one another's feet (John 13:14).

5. Don't be haughty: be of the same mind (Rom. 12:16).

6. Be subject to one another (Eph. 5:21).

7. Clothe yourselves in humility toward one another (1 Pet. 5:5).

Here are some more:

1. Do not judge one another, and don't put a stumbling block in another's way (Rom. 14:13).

2. Greet one another with a kiss (Rom. 16:16; 1 Cor. 16:20; 2 Cor. 13:12).

3. Husbands and wives: don't deprive one another of physical intimacy (1 Cor. 7:5).

4. Bear one another's burdens (Gal. 6:2).

5. Speak truth to one another (Eph. 4:25).

6. Don't lie to one another (Col. 3:9).

7. Comfort one another concerning the resurrection (1 Thess. 4:18).

8. Encourage and build up one another (1 Thess. 5:11).

9. Stimulate one another to love and good deeds (Heb. 10:24).

10. Pray for one another (James 5:16).
11. Be hospitable to one another (1 Pet. 4:9).

Those are a lot of references that emphasize the fact that we are better together. This is God's intention, His plan for us. And yet many of us are still looking for this kind of togetherness.

Recently in our community group, one of our families was struggling. The husband had served in Afghanistan, and as a result of chemical warfare, he was physically disabled. He, his wife, and their four children were about to be evicted from their rental home. Our group decided we could not sit idly by and watch this happen. We took up a collection and paid their rent for the month. When two of us met with the husband the following week to give them the money, he looked at us, dumbfounded. Then tears filled his eyes. "Why would you all do this?"

The man with me simply smiled. "That's what family does."

Does that type of family exist today? I believe it can. Let's talk about what it looks like next.

PRACTICAL QUESTIONS TO CONSIDER

1. What places do you see the "not me, but we" idea?

   _____

   _____

   _____

2. What places do you see courage and consideration put on display in equal fashion? Describe what happens.

   _____

   _____

   _____

3. Describe the characteristics of a good family.

_____

_____

_____

PUT IT INTO PRACTICE

Pick something you could do by yourself but would be better to do with someone else—and do it.

Maybe you could go visit an assisted living center. Instead of going alone, take someone with you. Perhaps you could take someone and serve a meal at the local shelter. Make an impact with someone else.

CHAPTER EIGHT

We Are Family

Families are like fudge—mostly sweet, with a few nuts.

Les Dawson

Some people say living the Christian life would be easier if it weren't for people. While that may feel like the truth sometimes, the reality is, being a "solo Christian" is not found in the New Testament. In the early church, people did life "together." Jesus talked about believers being known by their love for one another (John 13:34–35). To truly love someone, you have to be with them, not living in *isolation* or *insulation*. Being together is how God has wired us, and when we live that way, it will set us free. But why did people in the early church *accept* this accountability? What fueled their desire to submit to one another? How were they able to live in this kind of authenticity? The two qualities that enrich our one-to-one friendships also bind groups of people together for a common purpose, a shared vision.

Acts 2:42–47 uses the word *together* several times. The people ate **together,** prayed **together,** listened **together.** They did not live in isolation from one another. They also were not insulated from one another. Let's read it.

> They devoted themselves to the apostles' teaching and to fellowship, to the breaking of bread and to prayer. Everyone was filled with awe at the many wonders and signs performed by the apostles. All the believers were *together* and had everything in common. They sold property and possessions to give to anyone who had need. Every day they continued to meet *together* in the temple courts. They broke bread in their homes and ate *together* with glad and sincere hearts, praising God and enjoying the favor of all the people. And the Lord added to their number daily those who were being saved. (emphasis added)

Many people try to tackle life by themselves. But the Bible gives us intentional directions for the best way to do life. When Jesus's earthly ministry was over, He told the disciples He would send the Holy Spirit, and soon after the sending of the Holy Spirit, the church was established as God's vehicle for doing His work. The church is, or should be, family.

It Starts with Relationship

Sometimes we overlook the fact that the first followers of Jesus were friends with one another. Have you ever heard anyone say they wished for fewer, less-meaningful relationships? We all long to have more connectivity with friends. God created us this way. He placed this desire within us because He knew how it would benefit us.

What does the Bible say about friendship? The subject of friendship appears throughout the Bible, especially in John 15:12–15.

This is My commandment, that you love one another, just as I have loved you. Greater love has no one than this, that one lay down his life for his friends. You are My friends if you do what I command you. No longer do I call you slaves, for the slave does not know what his master is doing; but I have called you friends, for all things that I have heard from My Father I have made known to you. (NASB)

Have you ever thought about what the first *problem* in the world was? It was not sin, but solitude.[1]

Everything God did at creation, He pronounced as "good," but after He created Adam, there is a drastic change in the Lord's announcement. "It is *not good* for the man to be alone" (Gen. 2:18, emphasis added). Before the fall and before sin had entered the world, God said something was not good. When God created Adam, he was incomplete. Why? Because he needed companionship; he needed relationship.

Think about that for a moment. What does this tell us? Although our biggest problems today *are* sin and idolatry, *our first problem was that we were isolated and lonely.*[2]

Sister Sledge sang it well with their song "We Are Family." If you don't recognize the song, that's okay. The title speaks for itself. That sentiment applies to the church, or at least it should. The sisters and brothers of Christ make up the family of God. Now more than ever, people are looking for family.

Maybe you've visited churches and left because you could not find this "family" feeling. I've been in your shoes. It's disappointing. Some people say, "The family feel doesn't exist." I disagree. One of the key things that **should** exist in the church is *compassionate fellowship.*

Acts paints a picture of a vibrant fellowship, and it sounds much deeper than what we sometimes see in churches today. Is fellowship just getting together for a potluck meal? Is that all fellowship means, or is it just one part of fellowship?

Growing up in the South, I thought fellowship was a noun, a thing. Someone would announce "there's going to be a fellowship." And, of course, it always revolved around food. In fact, to make it alliterative, we always talked about *food, fun, and fellowship.* I thought these three things couldn't happen independently. When fellowship happened, we knew food and fun would be involved. For those of us who have in common a faith in Christ, the biblical word for this friendship and community is *fellowship.* The Greek word is *koinonia.* In other words, both people are working to make the relationship and friendship happen. The church at Leesburg understood this koinonia.

As I look back over the churches I have served or attended, I remember those Acts 2 times of compassionate fellowship. As I'm thinking about this, I realize that the times of fellowship I've experienced should have some comparison to the kind of fellowship Peter and John experienced in Acts 2. This fellowship should feel like family. Everyone should be able to see we are together, giving love in a family dose. *Compassionate fellowship is one of the benefits of doing life in community and is impossible if we live life alone.*

Gather around the Table

What creates the kind of fellowship we read about in Acts 2? I *do* like food. And the early church certainly did meet and eat a lot, almost as much as some Baptists I know. (I grew up Southern Baptist.) Something about eating together transforms the time people spend with each other.

During the small group in our home on Sunday evenings, we **always** have food. Sometimes we have a theme like Mexican or a "favorite soup" night or a baked potato bar. Sometimes it's a potluck. But food is always on the list. We read the Bible as a group and talk about what we read, but I've discovered something. The "real" conversations usually happen while we're eating. That's when the day-to-day life questions and answers get discussed. When it's time to read or study the Bible, we can sometimes pull out our "spiritual" answers. But eating relaxes us. Science tells us eating releases chemicals that make our bodies feel at ease. Not to mention, eating our favorite food puts us in a good mood too.

Food has a way of disarming us, allowing us to relax and enjoy the company of someone else. Maybe the early church was on to something. In our fast-paced world, few of us sit down to enjoy a meal together because we're so distracted with our "microwave" mentality. It took a lot longer to cook a meal in the days of the early church. In fact, social media is a lot like grabbing a snack on the go, whereas community is much more like sitting down and taking time to enjoy a large meal: perhaps an appetizer, the main meal, and a dessert to follow. It's interesting that to get that kind of meal in North America, you have to pay the big bucks. Maybe what you are paying for is the time you spend taking up the space in the restaurant more than the food you devour.

In our Sunday night group, we spend a lot of our time together preparing and setting out the meal, much more than a typical one-hour worship service. I've noticed that we tend to slow down. We take time to listen to one another. We find out what we have in common and what our differences might be. **Personal discovery**: if you feel like you are living life alone, the answer may be to *slow down*.

Slowing Down to Pray

Webster's defines *fellowship* as "companionship" or "company."[3] That sounds like the kind of fellowship Peter and John experienced. When you hear the word *companion* you don't think of people running in opposite directions. You think of people *doing stuff together.*

Acts 2 shows us another quality of compassionate fellowship: prayer. Prayer was their first instinct—not their last resort. They were devoted to prayer. Again, Webster's helps us here. To *devote* is to "give over or direct to a cause."[4] And the New American Standard translation reminds us they were "continually" devoting; it's not a one-and-done deal.

These early disciples prayed together. And they prayed for one another. Prayer is an intimate expression, and it requires spending time together. Yes, there should be personal time spent in prayer with God alone, but as a community, we need to be praying for one another as a group. It is one thing to pray for yourself, but have you ever experienced the connection of hearing someone else lift you and your needs before the Lord in prayer? What a powerful connection! How much time or resources do most of us give to the area of prayer?

One of the biggest statements of encouragement I can receive from a fellow believer is a genuine, "I am praying for you." Prayer is a bond like no other; it is the glue that held the early church together. Those who pray together stay together. (We'll talk more about this exciting benefit of community in a later chapter.)

Family Disagreements

Do you ever have family disagreements? Sure you do, and so do I. Most often our family disagreements revolve around picking a place to eat out. Isn't that ridiculous? The fact that we even get to eat out should make us happy. But with two college students in the family and a strong-willed mom and dad, we can wind up with four out of four different ideas on where to eat.

With different opinions, tastes, and personalities, we will never agree 100 percent about everything. And neither did the early believers. And yet, somehow, they continued to be unified, despite disagreements.

Acts 2:44 tells us all of the believers "were together and had all things in common" (NASB). I love that! Don't be confused here. The verse is not saying they all agreed. It's not saying they all liked the same things. They were not carbon copies of one another. They each had their own personalities and maintained their own individuality, but they were of *one* heart and *one* mind. How is that possible? I believe, in part, it's because they had the bigger picture in mind.

The people, that is, the church in Peter and John's day, saw the big picture because their focus was on the right person: Jesus. Notice they prayed and worshiped, and as a result of their focus, *compassionate fellowship happened.*

> Day by day continuing with one mind in the temple, and breaking bread from house to house, they were taking their meals together with gladness and sincerity of heart. (Acts 2:46 NASB)

Authentic worship and compassionate fellowship are inextricably woven together. One cannot happen without the other. They feed on each other. Compassionate fellowship produces authentic worship. And authentic worship is a breeding ground for compassionate fellowship. That's why worship with the body of Christ is so important. Individually worshiping God is important, of course, but it's not enough. There is so much joy experienced in gathering together with others in worship. We will talk more about this benefit later as well. The believers had *one* heart and *one* mind. Isn't that the kind of group you'd like to be a part of?

Learning Self-Denial?

For that kind of one heart and one mind to happen, self-denial is a critical component. It's not a term we use much today. Such a message won't draw a crowd. Why not?

Self-denial means I can't always have my way. Not having my way is the opposite of an entitlement mentality. Sometimes we may think self-denial is a bad thing, but without it, there is no way a *group* can be of *one* heart and *one* mind. Are you willing to deny yourself to allow for the wishes of someone else? Do you always have to get your way? Are you the one always being served?

I'm still working on this. But I think I've come a long way over the past several years. One of the things that really began to change my heart was the long-term international mission trips I've been blessed to be a part of. I've had the honor of seeing God at work in many countries, such as the Dominican Republic, Haiti, Bolivia, Brazil, and Malawi. In each of those trips, God took me by surprise. Schedules changed, transportation wasn't dependable, we were unable to meet at regular mealtimes, the amenities of indoor plumbing and/or heat and air-conditioning weren't always available. Even a decent place to sleep was sometimes a distant memory.

God used these experiences to break me and humble me. The things I thought I needed to survive were not really needs, they were "wants." Sometimes we—and I include myself in that we—have a big problem distinguishing between the two.

I think the people in Peter and John's day had the same problem. Acts 2 tells us that they shared everything they had. When someone had a need, the group met it. Do you belong to a community like that? Are there people around you who have needs that are going unmet? Have you seen your group provide for people in a phenomenal, God-like way? Have you ever been able to be a part of that? I have, and let me tell you, it is life changing.

Discovering Needs

Fellowship implies both giving and receiving. Yet, sometimes we think about fellowship only from the standpoint of receiving: What am I getting out of fellowship?

Fellowship is common participation in something, either by giving what you have to the other person or receiving what they have. Give and take is the essence of fellowship and is a key factor in the presence of quality in real community. This quality is what makes fellowship a huge benefit of doing life with others.

John teaches us that fellowship is two-dimensional. On one hand, it's vertical: "Our fellowship is with the Father and with his Son, Jesus Christ" (1 John 1:3). We can't have fellowship with one another until we have fellowship with the Father. So, if we are to have fellowship—true fellowship—with someone, we both need to have a growing relationship with the Father, or we aren't having fellowship, at least not as the Bible defines it.

On the other hand, the horizontal side of fellowship is the giving and receiving with one another that is birthed from our relationship and fellowship with the Father. We were created to have fellowship with God and one another.

People shared everything in the early church. If they saw someone in need, they met the need. If that kind of fellowship were the hallmark of our churches today, people would be lined up to get in. We could not keep people out. The Bible tells us the world will know we are His disciples by our love for one another (John 13:35).

Compassionate fellowship is *sharing*. It's putting the needs of someone else above our own. Do you see that kind of fellowship in your group? If so, what does it look like? How would you describe it? One of the wonderful things that happens when you do life with others is you are able to discover needs.

Not Alone

We were not created to live life alone. God gave us the cure for loneliness right from the beginning in the Garden of Eden. Our

Creator knew we needed company, companionship. In fact, our growth depends on it.

> Carry each other's burdens, and in this way you will fulfill the law of Christ. (Gal. 6:2)

> As iron sharpens iron,
>> so one person sharpens another. (Prov. 27:17)

> So in Christ we, though many, form one body, and each member belongs to all the others. (Rom. 12:5)

There are hundreds of Scriptures that talk about doing life with others. We can't grow without it. We need each other. God intended for us to live with real, true relationships. Life without friends or family isn't a pretty picture. Nor is life without real relationships. I want to be a part of a family, and that means enjoying the good and dealing with the bad. I want a community where I am accepted and loved. I need to be connected to other people who will help me grow, carry my burdens, and give me a place to belong. My soul needs authentic community, and God knew that when He created me.

If we follow God's design for our lives, there will be a lot fewer lonely people out there. We are made for connectivity. We are made for relationship. We are better together.

You may be ready for this kind of connection. Or you may still be hesitant. I get that.

Doing life together is hard. Building trust and camaraderie takes time. Perhaps that's why the early believers met often together. They knew that to establish rapport with each other they had to make time for one another. Building unity with people who are different from you is not a simple task. It requires a willingness of the heart. If you haven't seen or been a part of real friendship like this, maybe there are some roadblocks keeping you from it.

The roadblocks could be in your own life or in the life of your group. We'll take a look at how to overcome those roadblocks in the next chapter.

PRACTICAL QUESTIONS TO CONSIDER

1. How could you discover the needs of another person and do something about them?

_____

_____

_____

2. How often do you experience the kind of fellowship this chapter describes with someone over a meal? Have you ever invited someone to come to your home and have some time together over a meal? Has someone done that for you? What was it like?

_____

_____

_____

3. Is your life moving too fast to have real relationships? How can you slow things down to have meaningful relationships?

_____

_____

_____

PUT IT INTO PRACTICE

Find someone who needs conversation and invite them over for a meal. Be intentional about engaging with them and finding out about them. If they ask about bringing something, ask them to bring something that will allow both of you to prepare it. For example, ask them to bring the lettuce for a salad you can make together. You add the tomatoes, peppers, and croutons together once they arrive.

CHAPTER NINE

Overcoming Roadblocks
to Friendship

*If you live to be 100, I hope I live to be 100 minus 1
day, so I never have to live without you.*

A. A. Milne

I put down my fork after taking another bite of ginger chicken
and looked at my friend. He was struggling with phony
relationships. He wanted real friendship, but he was tired
of getting burned. I prepared myself for what was to come next.

"It's almost like what came first, the chicken or the egg? We're
made for community. We're made for relationship. And if we can
have a relationship that's connected by our faith, it takes real
friendship to a whole different level. Everyone wants to find someone with whom they can have an authentic and honest relationship.
But," I said, jabbing another piece of the chicken with my fork,
"no one wants to be the person to have to put forth the effort. So,

until someone steps up and exerts some energy for friendship and genuine relationship, it won't happen."

My friend nodded in agreement.

"So, what are you going to do about it?" I asked.

It's one thing to talk about friendship and connectivity with other people. It's another thing to accomplish it. It's not easy, and it will require work. Relationships can't be one-sided. So, what are those things that seem to be roadblocks to this friendship we are all desiring? Let's look at some roadblocks that hinder this genuine fellowship and friendship. The reality is, some of them are individual things we can do something about. Some of them may be on the part of the other person.

Roadblock #1: Selfishness/Pride

When we were kids, if we had something that was ours, more than likely there was a time when we shouted, "Mine!" It's what children do *until* they learn how to share. When a child screams "Mine!" it's one thing, but when an adult acts that way, it's another thing. Many churches are "mine fields." The thing that keeps true fellowship from happening is the unwillingness to eliminate the "mines."

Maybe you feel like it's your turn to have your way. Maybe you're even justified in wanting your way on a certain issue. But the reality is, we have to learn to share at some point. And sharing means being willing to let someone else have his or her way. That's hard. Sometimes I don't feel like sharing or letting someone else have their way—especially when I'm fairly certain my way is best. However, at times when I've "caved" and gone with the other person's wishes, I've learned that while my way is fine, sometimes another way is too.

I've also learned that when we focus on Jesus Christ, true fellowship and friendship can happen.

99

People shared everything in the early church. If they saw someone in need, they met the need. How awesome would it be if that kind of fellowship were the hallmark of our churches? A friend who is not a believer recently told me, "I don't have any problem believing you love those outside the church. What I don't know is if you will love me once I come in." What a sad commentary.

> Pride goes before destruction,
> a haughty spirit before a fall. (Prov. 16:18)

Pride centers on self. It runs totally contradictory to allowing real fellowship to happen. And yet it runs rampant in our churches, because it runs rampant in individuals. Pride says we always have to be right; pride convinces us our way is the only way. When you think about it, pride is the root of every sin. Pride is when we desire our way above all else. (The middle letter in PRIDE is an *I*. Interesting that the middle letter in SIN is an *I* as well.)

Roadblock #2: Jealousy

A second possible roadblock to fellowship and friendship is jealousy. Jealousy is pride's sibling. Jealousy usually breeds resentment against a perceived rival, a person enjoying success or advantage, or another's success or advantage itself. Jealousy can creep into any relationship. Jealousy, too, begins as a "mine field."

Why would you or I be resentful when someone else succeeds? Don't allow jealousy to take root in your heart. In churches where true fellowship is happening, you won't see jealousy or pride at work. This roadblock has been knocked down to allow God's Spirit to powerfully and freely flow.

Maybe you have heard the story about two shopkeepers who were bitter rivals. Their stores were directly across the street from each other, and they spent each day keeping track of each other's business. If one got a customer, he smiled in triumph at his rival and vice versa.

One night an angel appeared to one of the shopkeepers in a dream and said, "I will give you anything you ask, but whatever you receive, your competitor will receive twice as much. Would you be rich? You can be very rich, but he will be twice as wealthy. Do you wish to live a long and healthy life? You can, but his life will be longer and healthier. What is your desire?"

The man frowned, thought for a moment, and then said, "Here is my request: strike me blind in one eye!"

That illustration sounds ludicrous, but it happens every day. Jealousy clouds our judgment. It keeps us from experiencing true fellowship. Perhaps the best way to understand jealousy is to look at someone with the opposite trait.

> For many years Sir Walter Scott was the leading literary figure in the British Empire. No one could write as well as he. Then the works of Lord Byron began to appear, and their greatness was immediately evident. Soon an anonymous critic praised [Lord Byron's] poems in a London paper. [The critic] declared that in the presence of these brilliant works of poetic genius, Scott could no longer be considered the leading poet of England. It was later discovered that the unnamed reviewer had been none other than Sir Walter Scott himself![1]

Talk about humility. Sir Walter Scott lifted up a fellow writer and was expressing gratitude for his gift. Oh, that the church would open her eyes and applaud the good works of God's people without considering who will get the credit. The opposite of jealousy is humility.

> I am reminded that when we humble ourselves, He will lift us up. (James 4:10, author's paraphrase)

Roadblock #3: Unforgiveness

The third roadblock to fellowship and friendship happens a lot today. It's a familiar story and it starts when someone gets offended. Somebody forgot a birthday, or a friend said something inappropriate, and people get upset and then leave. Unforgiveness is everywhere. Unforgiveness that is not dealt with will lead to bitterness and malice and rage. It will eat at you from the inside out, thereby producing negative effects on your health and diminishing your joy. A lot of problems we see in the world today have unforgiveness at the root. How dangerous is unforgiveness? It's deadly!

Matthew 6:14–15 (ESV) says, "For if you forgive others their trespasses, your heavenly Father will also forgive you, but if you do not forgive others their trespasses, neither will your Father forgive your trespasses."

To get better at forgiveness, I practice forgiveness. No matter what the cost, I let go of the past. I realize that sometimes it is easier said than done, but we must be willing to do it. Forgiveness is more freeing for us than for the one who needs the forgiveness.

Here's a story of a father and son in Spain who were estranged:

The son ran away, and the father set off to find him. He searched for months to no avail. Finally, in a last desperate effort to find him, the father put an ad in a Madrid newspaper. The ad read: Dear Paco, meet me in front of this newspaper office at noon on Saturday. All is forgiven. I love you. Your Father. On Saturday 800 Pacos showed up, looking for forgiveness and love from their fathers.[2]

We all long for forgiveness. If unforgiveness is in your heart or in your group, there will never be true fellowship. Do you need forgiveness? Is there anyone whom you need to forgive?

Roadblock #4: Disunity

The fourth roadblock to fellowship and friendship is what Oxford's calls *disunity*. This is defined as having "disagreement and conflict within a group."[3]

Obviously, disunity is the opposite of unity. We see it played out every day in almost every avenue of life. During a game, we see players arguing with one another or even coaches and players getting into it about a play gone wrong. It happens in the business world. An employee works as hard as they can but is never able to please the boss. Disunity in our faith community should be unacceptable to us. It's a roadblock that prevents the church from winning in its mission. It's also a black eye on the face of the church for all the community to see, and it halts the progress of the church.

Unfortunately, disunity is a widespread problem. People who are supposed to be working together, playing on the same team, aren't unified about how to get the job done. Granted, there are many reasons disunity occurs. Sometimes it's due to a lack of quality leadership or is caused by a person who has lost focus on the task to be accomplished. Disunity keeps groups and organizations from achieving their potential.

Roadblock #5: We Don't Understand Submission

Dr. Matthew Vander Wiele says, "The essence of biblical community submits the individual to the community, not the community to the individual."[4] This is foreign to our modern Christian culture. What do we mean by an individual submitting to the community? To put it simply, the individual puts the community above his or her wishes or needs. Take church and small groups, for example. Do we go to small group with an attitude or expectation of getting

103

something out of it? Or is our attitude, "What can I contribute? How can I share something that will help someone else?"

If something more important comes up at the time when the small group is meeting, do we choose to put the small group on the back burner and go with the other activity, or do we choose to be consistent and be there for the relationships and friendships we're in the process of building? *God desires that you and I submit to our relationship with the believers to which He has led us.* If we have chosen to be a part of a specific community, we need to show up when that community of believers has decided to meet. Basically, we need to ask ourselves, "Are we putting the needs of others first?"

These are hard questions, I know. Let's ask God's guidance when it comes to tackling this area of submission. Jesus was big on fellowship. He knew that when His followers experienced fellowship the bonds of unity would be strengthened. He also knew unity would be very important for us to make it through this life. In fact, one of His final prayers for us was that we would be unified:

> My prayer is not for them alone. I pray also for those who will believe in me through their message, that all of them may be one, Father, just as you are in me and I am in you. May they also be in us so that the world may believe that you have sent me. I have given them the glory that you gave me, that they may be one as we are one—I in them and you in me—so that they may be brought to complete unity. Then the world will know that you sent me and have loved them even as you have loved me. (John 17:20–23)

Overcoming Roadblocks

Overcoming roadblocks like these is not for the faint of heart. It also takes the determination of a man or woman of substance who decides the togetherness God calls us to is vitally important.

Fellowship is heaven, and lack of fellowship is hell:
Fellowship is life, and lack of fellowship is death:
And the deeds that ye do upon the earth,
It is for fellowship's sake that ye do them.[5]

Are you ready to rid your life of the roadblocks that prevent true fellowship and friendship? If you are, you will be on the road to discovering how we can be better together.

To get there may mean we have to mature—that is, grow up.

PRACTICAL QUESTIONS TO CONSIDER

1. How can you help demonstrate compassionate fellowship?

2. Have you ever been the recipient of compassionate fellowship? How did it make you feel?

3. What acts of selflessness have you seen in the life of a fellow believer that demonstrated a real heart for fellowship?

4. What roadblocks to fellowship have you experienced? What did you do about it?

_____

_____

_____

PUT IT INTO PRACTICE

Here are some ways you can put fellowship into practice.

Our neighborhood has a Facebook group. Why not invite a group of neighbors over to your house for a soup social and get to know each other? That's an easy way to see who likes company and who likes soup while at the same time building community.

Spread the word on your Nextdoor online community about a book club. Pick a book that could spark conversation, and invite people to participate in a four-week discussion of the book. If you don't use the Nextdoor app, post a message on your neighborhood's social media page or ask your neighborhood leader if you can put something in the next bulletin.

Invite friends who like movies to get together and show an animated movie at your neighborhood clubhouse for families with children. If you don't have a clubhouse, see if there are some families who would offer their home and set up a rotation to do this in various homes in your community. That's a great way to meet your neighbors and provide a free night of entertainment for families with children. You get to be the hero and build community at the same time.

CHAPTER TEN

Learning to Trust

> The best way to find out if you can trust somebody
> is to trust them.
>
> Ernest Hemingway

I was tired, it was late, and I thought I would veg out by watching something on the tube. I scanned through the television stations looking for something that might help me fall asleep. Boy, was that a mistake. After ten minutes, I found myself wound back up again, irate, and wanting to stick the remote in the garbage disposal.

There were debates about some issue on every one of the major news networks. The debates were important, as were the issues, but that's not what sickened me. What made me want to throw my Doritos at the television set was the way supposedly "mature," "educated" adults were arguing with one another like toddlers fighting over a piece of candy. There was no calm, articulate, give-and-take conversation. There was no courage, and, for sure, no consideration for the other person speaking. My wife walked back into the den just as I yelled, "Grow up!" to the TV screen. (Yes, I know they couldn't hear me, and yelling at the television might be considered immature, but these people were being unbelievably ridiculous.) I decided to turn off the set and save the remote.

If we want to do life together with others, it will require us to grow up. Not just physically, but emotionally, mentally, and most of all, spiritually. We don't talk about that much these days, but we should always be maturing spiritually. If we know Jesus and have a personal relationship with Him, He should be our role model. Each day, there should be a growing consistency of looking more and more like Jesus. The big "churchy" word here is *sanctification*.

There's a scary theology that seems to be sweeping Christendom. There are some who would say God's grace is everything and, because of it, I should cease striving. To those dear friends, I would say this. I want to live a life that is a consistent representation of Jesus. I am not striving to earn His favor or acceptance. I am striving to be like Him because I want other people to be drawn to Him. James talks about this when he says, "Faith without deeds is dead" (James 2:26). If I am not growing in maturity as a believer, then I need to take a hard look at my salvation experience.

Accountability Is Real Relationship

We talked a little about accountability earlier, but it might help us to go a little deeper. We tend to see accountability as having a "hall monitor" to help us stop doing bad things. That's the foundation of my accountability with my trainer, Mike. I wanted to stop eating unhealthy food and get in better shape, and Mike helped, but he was more than a hall monitor. We shouldn't reduce spiritual growth to quitting the bad things in our lives. Allowing sin into our lives is an important issue. But omitting the things God has called us to do matters as well. "When we reduce holiness to simply 'stop sinning,' we become incredibly superficial and miss the big picture of what Christ's salvation is really all about—transformation,"[1] says Jayson Bradley.

So, what is biblical accountability? It's when love is not reduced to "monitoring" one another. That's not a true reflection of biblical love. Bradley goes on to say, "When we're embedded in a culture that equates accountability and love, it's no wonder we believe we love the culture by judging it."[2]

True friends trust one another. When we don't trust each other, we'll never be transparent. A true spiritual friendship's goal is unconditional love. When friends have this kind of love, neither is shocked when the other fails to live up to a Christian standard. But it's also true that neither friend reinforces the notion that failure diminishes God's acceptance of us. A true spiritual friendship contains elements of accountability, of course. But that's not the defining characteristic. That's only part of the picture.[3]

> Spiritual friends help each other recognize God's movement and promptings. They encourage each other to stay connected to the vine so that they may produce fruit. And while there may be times these kinds of friends need to say tough things to each other, it's always with a sense of humility and love [that is birthed in trust and friendship].[4]

We often treat relationships as a commercial transaction. Meaning, we befriend for the benefits we receive. My friend Mike was not just concerned with the benefits of working out and losing weight, even though those were *my* benefits. It wasn't a contractual relationship. It was more covenantal. Proverbs teaches us about "a friend who sticks closer than a brother" (18:24). It commands us, "Do not forsake your friend" (27:10).

Scripture frequently mentions accountability. Hebrews 10 talks about how as believers we can encourage one another when we are "together." Ecclesiastes 4:9–12 says,

> Two are better than one, because they have a good reward for their toil. For if they fall, one will lift up his fellow. But woe to him who is alone when he falls and has not another to lift him up! Again, if two lie together, they keep warm, but how can one keep warm alone? And though a man might prevail against one who is alone, two will withstand him—a threefold cord is not quickly broken. (ESV)

When we are accountable to others, it can help us face spiritual warfare (Eph. 6:12). I know many proud military men and women who are grateful to know that someone has their back in battle. It is the same thing spiritually. I have many friends like this who help me stay connected. My connection with them helps me stay connected with God.

We are reminded of God's faithfulness and made aware of the power of forgiveness (1 John 1:9) when we confess our sins to one another (James 5:16). Being accountable to others opens us to life-giving truth and prevents us from hiding in the darkness of our own shame and challenges. Other Christians can support us in our walk with Christ by praying for us (James 5:16). What awesome gifts these are for doing life together!

Living the Christian life is difficult enough when we have people who walk with us. If we try to walk with God by ourselves, we're doomed to failure. That was never God's intention. Ultimately, we are accountable to God. But we are also accountable to one another as brothers and sisters in Christ. We are part of a **family** and part of the body. And doing life together enables us to grow. But all of this is birthed from genuine friendship.

How awesome it would be for people to see churches filled with authentic friendships! We know those friendships won't be perfect, but they can contain trust, forgiveness, and the genuine love of God. People will look at us and want to know the Jesus who makes those relationships possible.

That's what Jesus said in John 13:35: "By this all people will know that you are my disciples, if you have love for one another" (ESV). And later in this same conversation, Jesus defined this "love for one another" in terms of the mutual love of friends. He said, "This is my commandment, that you love one another as I have loved you" (15:12 ESV). And how has He loved us? "Greater love has no one than this, that someone lay down his life for his friends" (15:13 ESV). This is how we show the world that we are Jesus's disciples: when we love one another as He loved us—namely, with sacrificial friendship. Having that kind of accountability is wonderful! But there's another aspect that is a part of this relationship.

Authenticity Reexamined

I love the phrase "the ground is level at the foot of the cross," meaning that we each stand on equal footing at the cross. None of us is better than another, and we all need the salvation Christ offers. Acts 2 tells us that all the believers "were one in heart and mind." That doesn't mean they agreed on everything, but they valued the opinions and thoughts of others. They pushed aside, apparently, petty differences for the sake of unity. We could learn a lot from their example. We need to learn respectful listening and disagreement. We seem to be more concerned with being right than being in close relationships. That's a dangerous place. This doesn't mean we don't stand up for what is right, but sometimes our presentation needs some improvement.

Jesus was the Master Teacher. He knew how to make people feel valued even when they were wrong. And He was always more concerned about their having a relationship with Him than proving He was right. The early believers understood this idea, because

Paul's instruction in Romans 12:3 reminded every believer not to think of himself more highly than he ought to think. I'm grateful that I've found a group with whom there is equal footing.

The early church did life together. They had real relationships. They had families and conflicts and everything else you can think of. They lived in real communities. People had more opportunity to know each other. There was no hiding. There was no insulating yourself from those around you.

Contrast that to today, when people live and work and go to school far from a community. We drive into our neighborhoods, raise our garage doors, pull inside, then lower the door. Though we may live in something we call a "community," it doesn't mean community exists.

When we experience community and do life together, we learn from one another and discover insights that come from other believers. They can challenge our interpretation of Scripture and we can challenge theirs. Our fellow believers can be a filter for us to discern God's voice and to live an authentic Christian life. When we are separated from other believers, we are much more susceptible to sin, temptation, and being led astray. Just like a single sheep separated from the flock is more likely to be harmed, we are protected and more secure when we are together.

Life gets real in relationship with others. God often uses relationships to make us grow and to prune us, whether it's helping us realize we were wrong about an issue, helping us learn to forgive someone, or helping us deal with someone's personality or beliefs. In relationship with others, we learn to serve and love well.

But my favorite reason for choosing not to live life solo is because it's hard to receive encouragement when you do so. Hebrews 10:24–25 says, "And let us consider how to stir up one another to love and good works, not neglecting to meet together, as is the habit of some, but encouraging one another, and all the more as you see the Day drawing near" (ESV).

Being encouraged helps us live an authentic life. Living the Christian life in a world that is running in the opposite direction will always wear us down. Let me give you an example of someone I've seen exemplify accountability and authenticity.

A Personal Example

Sam Davis was my youth pastor. When I met Sam, he'd been in ministry for quite a few years. He's the person God sent to our church just as I was thinking this "Christianity thing" was not really for me. I was a sophomore in high school and saw a lot of students who claimed to be Christians living a double life—they would get drunk on Friday night and talk about how great God was on Sunday morning.

I thought there had to be more to Christianity than that.

Sam took me and a handful of other guys in the youth group to an event at Anderson University in Anderson, South Carolina, called Key Youth Week. There was great music and recreation, and the messages I heard from the Scriptures were phenomenal as well. But what made the deepest impression on me was seeing people genuinely striving to live for Jesus. I left that event changed because of the leadership that had been exemplified at the conference and birthed in the context of this small group of high school guys. But the benefit really flourished when I returned and joined some other high school students for Bible study and fellowship in Sam's home every Tuesday night for the next two years.

One of the things I learned from watching Sam was the attitude and work ethic of a servant. He and I were often the last ones to leave the church after an event. One night I had a rather lackadaisical attitude about cleaning up. As a result, the place wasn't as clean as it should have been.

Sam didn't hesitate to make that a teachable moment. "We always want to leave things better than when we found them," he said. "Someone else may need to use the room when we're finished."

That attitude—consistently striving to honor God—permeated his work and ministry . . . and my heart.

Everyone knew Sam would finish what he started and do his best to make sure it was done right. As a teen, I took note of that quality and determined to emulate it. A few extra minutes to do things right always resulted in fruit in more ways than one could count. Although cleaning a room was something people could see, it was still a reflection of Sam Davis's inner character. Character that screamed *integrity*.

Sam was purposeful in modeling and mentoring. Most of us get "too busy" to mentor those around us. If we don't invest in others who are coming up behind us, the church will fail to grow and fall short of being what God intended it to be.

When we don't share with others the lessons we have learned, we are basically throwing those lessons away. What an incredible waste. When we mentor those coming up behind us, they get our wisdom, and we get the joy of passing down something that will help someone else. It's not just a responsibility but a *benefit* of doing life with other people. Do you have anyone in your life who has demonstrated characteristics like these that make it easier to trust?

PRACTICAL QUESTIONS TO CONSIDER

1. Do you have anyone to whom you are accountable? Not just someone who "keeps score," but a friend who loves

you unconditionally and cares enough about you to tell you the truth? If not, who might be such a friend? Are you that kind of friend for someone?

_____

_____

_____

2. What words come to mind when you think about living authentically?

_____

_____

_____

PUT IT INTO PRACTICE

Now it's time to start getting serious. Are you ready to invest in life-changing relationships?

Are you ready for authentic and accountable relationships? The challenge for you this week is to pray and find one person with whom you can begin this kind of relationship.

CHAPTER ELEVEN

The Power of Praying Together

Prayer does not change God, but it changes him who prays.

Søren Kierkegaard

The pastor stood up, and instead of beginning his sermon, he asked if anyone needed prayer. One by one hands went up across the auditorium, and almost immediately people began to move. I wasn't sure what was happening since I was a visitor on this day. So, I sat and watched. My heart began to overflow with joy as I watched people go and stand beside those whose hands were raised. Groups of people surrounded each person who needed prayer, placing their hands on those individuals and praying for them together. I had never seen anything like this before.

I began to hear a few people weeping as the prayers of those around them continued. And the pastor stood at the pulpit, praying silently. I sat in amazement at the culture that had been created in that church. When someone needed prayer, fellow believers sprang into action and surrounded their brothers and sisters and began to bring the needs of the person to the Lord. What a beautiful picture!

Those who pray together stay together.

Maybe you've heard that statement before. And it's true. Prayer is an intimate form of communication, made even more so when it's you, God, and someone else praying together. Prayer connects us to God, obviously; but there are other reasons to pray and other benefits of prayer.

Having someone you can pray with is a sign you have a strong friendship and relationship. And those kinds of relationships were the foundation of the early church. Their intimacy came through times of fellowship and worship.

One of the best ways to get to know a fellow believer is to pray together. In our communication with God we are most likely to let the walls down and be who we really are. In prayer, we are able to reveal our hearts in a way like no other. Timothy Keller quotes Jack Miller, a friend and pastor, on praying together: "You can tell if a man or woman is really on speaking terms with God."[1]

I remember sitting in my office with some of my friends and colleagues. We had gathered to pray like we often did, but for some reason, on this particular occasion, God was really dealing with me. I had a lot on my mind and several important decisions to make. And when it came my turn to pray, I could only mutter a few words before I began to weep in front of my friends. I could sense them lifting their heads and looking up at one another, wondering what was going on with me. And in the same moment, I felt their hands on my shoulder assuring me of their presence and support. This freedom to be authentic came as a result of praying together. There are many times in our lives when praying together is exactly what God wants us to do. In fact, it might be that sometimes God only answers certain prayers when they are prayed together. We did finish praying together that day, and my friends realized my tears were because of my amazement at the power of prayer.

Prayer Unifies

> Is anyone among you sick? Let him call for the elders of the church, and let them pray over him, anointing him with oil in the name of the Lord. And the prayer of faith will save the one who is sick, and the Lord will raise him up. And if he has committed sins, he will be forgiven. Therefore, confess your sins to one another and pray for one another, that you may be healed. The prayer of a righteous person has great power as it is working. (James 5:14–16 ESV)

Prayer is a unifying agent in the life of a believer and in the health of a group of believers. We need unity and to be in "one accord" as the early believers were, and as we pray together, that unity is increased. After all, it's hard to be in disunity with someone when you are praying regularly with that person.

Prayer allows God's glory to be known more widely because multiple people have been involved in bringing their petitions and requests to the Father. The Bible tells us "if two of you agree on earth about anything they ask, it will be done for them by my Father in heaven" (Matt. 18:19 ESV). There is added power when we unite with brothers and sisters in Christ to join our hearts and make our collective requests to our Father.

Before I go on a mission trip, I recruit people to be a part of my mission experience. Many times, I ask them to contribute financially (because a financial investment seems to make people more interested in the trip itself), but many times I ask people to be a part of my prayer team. The fantastic thing about this is that when I post pictures on social media and give a report when I return home, those who have prayed or given financially get to celebrate with me when they hear what God has done. They were a part of the trip even though they were unable to take the journey with me. By being involved prayerfully, they are allowed to participate in seeing God's hand at work. We are part of the mission effort . . . together.

Prayer is also vitally connected to worship. Worship invites the presence and power of the Holy Spirit into our midst when we pray together, and when the Spirit of God is present, wonderful things happen. People begin to hear the Lord speak to them. The church in Antioch saw this: "While they were worshiping the Lord and fasting, the Holy Spirit said, 'Set apart for me Barnabas and Saul for the work to which I have called them.' So after they had fasted and prayed, they placed their hands on them and sent them off" (Acts 13:2–3). During a time of prayer and worship *together*, God gave important instructions to the people that monumentally transformed the world through the ministry of these two men.

Prayer is a benefit of doing life with other people. And prayer itself accomplishes a lot in our lives individually and collectively in our faith communities.

Praying Together Decreases Our Burdens

Praying with others lightens our load. Have you ever had a time when the burden you were carrying was so heavy that you had to share the load with someone else? If you have, then you understand another benefit of doing life together. Knowing someone else is praying for you and sharing a burden makes a tremendous difference.

I remember times when I have had to make an extremely difficult decision. I would pray about it alone. I would agonize over the decision. I would make a list of pros and cons on a piece of paper. But when I finally shared the concern with someone else, I

119

always felt better. Why? Because someone else had agreed to pray with me and to carry part of the burden. That's another reason we are better together.

> Share each other's burdens, and in this way obey the law of Christ. (Gal. 6:2 NLT)

Praying Together Decreases Our Doubt

Have you ever prayed about something but in the back of your mind been thinking, "God won't really answer this prayer" or "God isn't concerned with this prayer"? I have. And then I have had the opportunity to pray with someone else about the same issue and my doubt decreased dramatically. It's the power of two or more people connected to the Holy Spirit requesting the same thing from the Lord. "Again I say to you, that if two of you agree on earth about anything that they may ask, it shall be done for them by My Father who is in heaven. For where two or three have gathered together in My name, I am there in their midst" (Matt. 18:19–20 NASB).

Maybe it's our unity in prayer that helps us overcome our doubt?

When we pray, we need faith. We need to believe we will receive an answer to our prayer. Doubting and wavering hinders our faith. Praying with someone else will help us alleviate doubts so our faith is not hindered and we can receive from God.

Praying Together Increases Our Faith

If we don't pray with others, we may find ourselves lacking in faith. One of the main reasons our spiritual lives sometimes become stagnant is because we don't have other individuals with whom we can pray in faith. Faith grows as we pray together. Jeremiah

29:11–13 is a wonderful promise written to God's people: "'For I know the plans I have for you,' declares the LORD, 'plans to prosper you and not to harm you, plans to give you hope and a future. Then you will call upon me and come and pray to me, and I will listen to you. You will seek me and find me when you seek me with *all* your heart'" (emphasis added). Ecclesiastes also reminds us how important it is to be together:

> Two people are better off than one, for they can help each other succeed. If one person falls, the other can reach out and help. But someone who falls alone is in real trouble. Likewise, two people lying close together can keep each other warm. But how can one be warm alone? A person standing alone can be attacked and defeated, but two can stand back-to-back and conquer. Three are even better, for a triple-braided cord is not easily broken. (Eccles. 4:9–12 NLT)

There is strength in numbers, and the Bible reminds us that when one falls, the other can help them up. When we pray with others, it allows us to be transparent, which strengthens the trust in our relationships. When we hear others pray for our needs, it gives us much encouragement as well.

Praying Together Broadens Our Perspective

Have you ever been overwhelmed with your own trials and troubles? Have you ever prayed with someone and had them share their struggles or difficulties? When this happens, we are more acutely aware that we aren't on this journey alone. It causes us to look outside of ourselves and our own needs. Praying together will not only fend off selfishness, it can also help us minimize our own problems. When we see we're not alone in the challenges of life, we develop a concern for other people. Sympathy is good, but empathy is even better, and it comes from a deeper awareness of what others are facing.

There are a lot of benefits to prayer and praying together; I've just shared a few here. But to enjoy these benefits we have to be willing to step out in friendship and relationship with others. Are you enjoying the benefit of someone else praying with you and for you? If not, can I encourage you to take a step in that direction today? I promise you that you will never regret it. And when you enter into a relationship with someone with whom you can pray, the awareness that you receive might just cause you to do some crazy and bizarre things. I'll share more about that in the next chapter.

PRACTICAL QUESTIONS TO CONSIDER

1. Who in your life can share your burdens?

2. Are you someone whom others can allow to carry a burden?

3. Discuss how you have experienced the power of sharing in prayer with another. How has this made you better together? How has this made you feel less lonely?

4. If you aren't enjoying the benefit of praying together with someone else, what prevents you from experiencing this?

_____

_____

_____

PUT IT INTO PRACTICE

For the next seven days, keep a prayer journal, writing down your prayers each day. At the end of the seven days, go back and see where God has answered, has brought confirmation, or has yet to answer your prayer. See if your perspective on any of your burdens has changed.

CHAPTER TWELVE

The Joy of Meeting Needs

Every faculty you have, your power of thinking or of moving your limbs from moment to moment, is given you by God. If you devoted every moment of your whole life exclusively to His service, you could not give Him anything that was not in a sense His own already.

C. S. Lewis

I pulled into the coffee shop like on any other Friday. Determined to get my cup of sweet tea and pull out my laptop to work for a while, I hopped out of the car with a smile on my face. This local establishment called Java Bistro has become a favorite of mine; the food is good, but the staff have become friends. It's a gathering spot in the community. As I walked up to place my order, I had already picked out my seat by the window where I intended to get to work on a few items for the day.

A familiar face greeted me at the counter. Connie took my order, handed me my tea, and said, "I'll be out in just a minute—I need to talk to you." Connie, a single grandmother who is raising her grandson alone, has become a friend. After a few minutes, she brought my food out, and I pushed my laptop to the side to give her my attention. "I need a car, so if you know anyone who might be willing to help me get one, please let me know."

She continued to talk, but honestly, I didn't hear much more after that. The only voice I heard was the thunderous reverberation of the Holy Spirit speaking to my heart: "You need to give her your car, you need to give her your car." Connie finished her sentence, and I mumbled something to her, probably something like, "I will be praying for you about that," and she walked away. The voice of the Lord continued to reverberate in my head. I was so shaken, I got up from the table, walked out to my car, and drove home. I couldn't talk. Tons of thoughts, however, flooded my mind.

When I walked in the door, my wife could tell something was wrong by the look on my face, because she immediately asked what had happened. I sat down at the table to tell her, but I couldn't speak. I was so overcome with emotion that tears began to roll down my face.

"What happened?" she asked again. She was beginning to panic. I'm sure she thought something terrible had occured. Maybe she thought I had wrecked the car.

"I think we are supposed to give away the car," I finally muttered.

For the next few minutes, we talked about what I felt the Lord was saying. I told Lynette about the experience I had at the coffee shop, and she listened as tears ran down my cheeks. She agreed that giving the car away was what we needed to do. Then the phone rang.

"Jack," the voice on the other end said, "are you coming back to the restaurant?"

"I can," I replied. "Why?"

The voice on the phone was Connie. "You left your laptop, backpack, and sweet tea on the table."

I ran out the door and headed back to the restaurant.

It's funny how the enemy can try to talk you out of something, especially when he knows he has limited time. The mile-or-so jaunt back to the coffee shop wasn't long enough for him to change my mind. I pulled into the parking space right in front to see Connie sweeping off the front walk. As I stepped out of the car with the keys in my hand, I knew who the new owner of my 2004 Ford Explorer was soon to be. As I handed her the keys that day, we both wept. Connie wept in celebration of receiving a vehicle. I wept because for the first time in a while, I got to experience the joy of meeting someone else's needs. It is one of the richest benefits of not doing life alone—being able to *know* about and meet the needs of other people. The benefit of fellowship we talked about earlier leads to the benefit of understanding real stewardship and the privilege and joy of meeting the needs of others.

Unfortunately, in a culture where most of us live alone (perhaps not physically, but alone in every other way—emotionally, psychologically, mentally, socially, spiritually), it is sometimes virtually impossible to think about meeting the needs of others because we're oblivious to those needs. We don't have a watchful eye, meaning we're not looking with eyes of awareness. We aren't living life asking, "Whose needs can I meet today?"

I had a friend recently make an excellent point. He said, "I often hear people talking about the need for believers to be the hands and feet of Jesus. While that is true," he said, "we will never be the hands and feet of Jesus until we have the *eyes* of Jesus." Scripture reminds us that when Jesus *saw* the crowds, He was moved with compassion for them (Matt. 9:36). We need the eyes of Jesus. That kind of eyesight helps us understand that our resources aren't for us alone. When we have such vision, it affects our stewardship.

What Is Stewardship?

Many people think stewardship is having a budget and trying to get out of debt. Some think it's writing a check to the church each month. Some think it's taking care of the environment. But those things only scratch the surface of the biblical concept of stewardship. Being a steward means recognizing that everything you have belongs to God (Ps. 24:1). It belongs to God because God created it all (Gen. 1:1). Being a steward means recognizing the huge responsibility of managing the things God has entrusted to us.

The early church understood what it meant to be stewards. They trusted in God for their provision. They understood owners have rights; stewards have responsibilities. Let that sink in. This concept dramatically affected my way of thinking. When it came to the issue of giving, the early church was not reluctant or hesitant to share their possessions and resources with one another, because they understood they were merely stewards. When we understand that we aren't the owners of what we have, but merely temporary managers, our perspective changes and we learn to trust the Giver of those resources.

Stewardship Is Wise Money Management

A pastor friend told me this story. Their church had a special time of giving one Sunday. Instead of passing the offering plate down each aisle like they usually did, he decided to have people come down to the front to the communion table and place their offerings in the plates. People walked down to the front at the expected time and placed their monies in the collection plates. After several minutes, my pastor friend thought everyone was finished, until a nine-year-old boy slipped out of one of the back rows, easing past his parents.

Daniel came down the aisle with his piggy bank in tow. Under his arm, the little bank began to rattle with all the change inside. As he clinked his way to the front, all eyes were on this young man. People were chuckling, smiling, and taking photos on their phones. Some

127

were even shooting video. When he arrived at the front, he opened the bank and began to shake it mightily. The coins fell out and hit the table. Some rolled onto the floor, some into the offering plates. When Daniel was sure the piggy bank was empty, he held it up to the light and stuck his finger inside to pull out the paper money, throwing the crumpled wads of money into the plate. Assured his bank was empty, he returned the stopper and made his way back to his seat. All eyes followed his progress.

"Daniel, come here for a moment," my pastor friend called out to him. Since the young boy had the attention of the congregation, my friend decided to make the most of it, unaware of the profound wisdom that was about to come out of the boy's mouth. "Daniel, you emptied your entire piggy bank. Aren't you worried? I mean, you gave everything out of your bank."

Without hesitation, the young boy looked up at the pastor and said, "Nope, because my daddy will fill it up again!"

People began to chuckle, then all was quiet as they thought about the truth of the boy's words. "My daddy will fill it up again."

Living in biblical stewardship means surrendering your finances to God. Some of us have gotten so caught up in the American Dream that we have forgotten our responsibilities to our brothers and sisters in Christ, not to mention the rest of the world around us.

> Remember the LORD your God, for it is he who gives you the ability to produce wealth. (Deut. 8:18)

If you have walked away from the church because you haven't seen this kind of stewardship and love for one another, please give your brothers and sisters in Christ another chance. Or better yet, show them the way.

If we loved one another enough to sacrifice personal possessions for the well-being of someone else—wow!—our churches could not contain the people who'd want to come in. Giving like this requires self-denial. It requires putting the needs of others before yourself (Phil. 2:3). Stewardship is not ordering your finances in a way that you can spend whatever you want. It's ordering your life in such a way that God can spend *you* however He wants.[1]

> Stewardship means learning to focus our *time, money, and energy* on what will make the most impact for eternity. (Matt. 6:20, author's paraphrase)

> Whoever sows sparingly will also reap sparingly, and whoever sows bountifully will also reap bountifully. Each one must give as he has decided in his heart, not reluctantly or under compulsion, for God loves a cheerful giver. (2 Cor. 9:6–7 ESV)

The Great Honda Giveaway

Back in the mid-1990s, I was in full-time ministry. One of my dear friends on our ministry staff and I were both recent newlyweds, and we were both one-car families. And did I mention we were in full-time ministry?

He and I were juggling ministry trips and home life. It was a challenge with having only one vehicle. One day, our former Sunday school leader, Mr. Bill, gave us a call. "I'd like for the two of you to drive over to my home today if you have a minute," he said. My friend and I were puzzled but agreed. We knew and loved him very much, but we didn't talk as often as we used to. He'd never asked us to just stop by.

When we arrived, his wife invited us in.

After we were seated in the living room, Mr. Bill joined us. "Tell me what God is doing with you guys and your ministry," he said.

We talked for a while, and he asked if we had any needs right now. We named a few things, but I don't recall either of us saying anything about a car. Finally, he stood up and said, "Come outside with me."

As we walked out the front door, he pulled two sets of keys out of his pocket, then turned to us. "Guys, God has blessed us, and we have two more cars than we do drivers. We have been praying, and God told us to give each of you one of these cars." He pointed at a 1980-something Honda Prelude and a 1980-something Honda CRX.

"They aren't new," he said. "But they run well. They're Hondas, so they have room for another hundred thousand miles or so. They've been taken care of, and I'd like for you to have them. You guys can decide who gets what."

My friend and I stood there speechless. Mr. Bill had been paying attention, and in the process, he'd discovered my friend and I had a need. We'd not expressed our need to anyone, and yet, here he was taking care of both of us.

A real demonstration of stewardship!

I want to be this kind of steward. Giving is contagious. I learned stewardship from my parents. I saw it demonstrated. I've been on the receiving end and have benefited greatly. And since I want to make an impact for the kingdom of God, I know one way I can do that is by being a good steward.

We learn how to do this when we're together with other people. Sometimes it means affording someone the opportunity to meet my needs as well. This support for one another should be the trademark of our lives and our churches. This kind of heart connection can be happening in all of our faith communities if we have the right focus. But sometimes our focus is on something else.

The Family Meeting

In 2011, my son, Will, and my daughter, Lauryn, who were nine and eleven at the time, joined my wife and me for our first international mission trip *together*. We traveled to Puerto Plata in the Dominican Republic to minister to a wonderful group of people. (I will share the prompting of this trip in a later chapter.) Since Will was young, he naturally connected with children his age. He had a great time playing with them but also sharing his testimony and doing crafts with them during the Bible camps in the villages. He was impacted in a profound way by the friendships he forged during that week on the ground in the third world, as was my daughter, Lauryn.

Lauryn connected instantly with the young girls. I was amazed at how this soon-to-be teenager started picking up the Spanish language that week. She quickly made friends with the young girls in the village. She enjoyed making crafts and singing with them as well. It was a challenge getting both of my kids on the plane to come back home.

Not too many days after we returned, Will asked my wife and me for a "family meeting." We smiled at the idea that our nine-year-old son was calling a family meeting, but we obliged. As we sat around the kitchen table that night, he told us he wanted to get rid of everything in his room. At first, I was a little shocked, but I also knew this was coming from what he'd seen in the DR. When I asked him why, he replied, "Because I don't really *need* those things. The kids in the Dominican Republic don't have those things, and I don't need them either." I told him that his mom and I would talk about it and let him know our decision in the morning.

The next morning, we sat down with him and told him he could get rid of everything except for his bed, because he needed a good night's sleep for school each day. He agreed to our compromise, and we were satisfied as well. Fast-forward almost nine years later, and would you like to know the only thing still in his room? His bed.

Why did he do it? To show God he was serious about following His Word. And by doing it, he dealt a deathblow to the spirit of greed that wreaks so much havoc in our world. I am proud of his heart to be a good steward of what God has given him. He is intentional about how he spends his money, because he knows all he has been given was given to him by the Lord. He learned this valuable lesson from being in community with other believers and serving. And he reminded our whole family too.

Stewardship Is Wise Time Management

Socrates warned, "Beware the barrenness of a busy life."

Stewardship is not just about money. It's also about how we spend our time. Or as I like to say, how we **invest** our time. It's hard to invest in people if we aren't connected in community. As a matter of fact, it's impossible. Only by doing life together are we able to make those investments.

> Be very careful, then, how you live—not as unwise but as wise, making the most of every opportunity, because the days are evil. (Eph. 5:15–16)

What would you say if you saw someone burning a pile of money? What if you saw them igniting five-, ten-, and twenty-dollar bills? You'd say that person is crazy. But when we squander time, it is like burning money in the sense that we're wasting it and not investing it.

> Go to the ant, you slacker!
> Observe its ways and become wise.
> Without leader, administrator, or ruler,
> it prepares its provisions in summer;
> it gathers its food during harvest.
> How long will you stay in bed, you slacker?
> When will you get up from your sleep? (Prov. 6:6–9 HCSB)

I mentioned earlier that part of the challenge of building relationships is our inability to make time for them. God has given us all the same amount of time: 86,400 seconds in a day. Time is something we take for granted these days. We spend hours watching TV or playing games on our mobile phones or checking social media, and we think this is normal. We spend hours stuck in traffic or standing in the checkout line. This is time we can never get back. Every second counts, and we should think about how we plan to spend them. How can we best use our time to make an impact in our families, jobs, and communities?

Here's the point: your priority determines the capacity of your life.

> Therefore, be careful how you walk, not as unwise men but as wise, making the most of your time, because the days are evil. (Eph. 5:15–16 NASB)

The phrase "making the most of your time" is translated in some versions of the Bible as "redeeming the time." In the original Greek language, *redeeming* is a word that means "to buy out of the market."[2] It refers to buying something valuable or important. The word *time* is not talking about chronology; it's the word *kairos*, which means "opportunity."[3]

Kairos is an appointed time in the purpose of God—it's a window of opportunity when one can act.

We need to make the most of the opportunity of time that God has given to us, and that starts with prioritizing what's important. We do this by asking God to help us steward the time we have each day to make an impact that is long-lasting, not fleeting or temporary.

Until we're able to manage our time well, we won't have time for the relationships our souls long for. Some of us have been running on the treadmill of life for so long, we think this is normal. But do you want to settle for that kind of normal?

What about you? What's God asking you to do about your time?

Stewardship Is Wise Talent Management

Stewardship also includes the gifts and talents God has given us. "As each has received a gift [we are to] use it to serve one another, as good stewards of God's varied grace" (1 Pet. 4:10 ESV).

God has given you a specific gift or gifts. He didn't give them to you haphazardly or by accident. God intentionally gifted you the way He did. Your gifts are not a result of genetics or experience but a strategic method to bless others and to connect, like puzzle pieces, to other people—to be interconnected. God doesn't give us gifts and talents to increase our significance but so we can use them for His purposes as we live in community.

This is a brilliant idea from God. If you look at faith communities that are operating effectively, you will notice many using the gifts they have in cooperation with one another. Where I'm not gifted, someone else might be. Where someone else is lacking a gift, I might be the one to have that gift. As members of the body, we complement one another. How awesome is our God to arrange such a thing!

It's a phenomenal blessing and gift from God to do life together. And when we channel our stewardship in the right direction, we will be in awe of what transpires. When a group of people, a faith community, is stewarding all their resources in the same direction—something marvelous happens. We will talk about that next.

PRACTICAL QUESTIONS TO CONSIDER

1. When has someone met a need for you that you know cost them something?

_____

_____

_____

2. When did you meet someone's need at a price to you?

3. Describe your perspective on stewardship.

4. Which of your gifts could be used more powerfully in the context of community?

PUT IT INTO PRACTICE

Take some time today at a restaurant, mall, or coffee shop and watch people. See if you can identify any needs that people may have. Think, hypothetically, what it might take for you to meet the needs of the people you see.

I promise that when you start thinking this way, you will be on the path to solving loneliness.

CHAPTER THIRTEEN

Rally around a Cause

> After they prayed, the place where they were meeting
> was shaken. And they were all filled with the Holy
> Spirit.
>
> Acts 4:31

I n September 2010, I traveled to Mozambique, Africa, with
a ministry that works with AIDS orphans. As we drove out
through the sand and trees on our way to visit these children,
I had no idea what I might see. The missionary leader had told
us we were going to make a stop to see a sibling group of three
children. For several hours we drove down a cattle path that finally
turned into a creek bed. At this point, the driver stopped the jeep
and mumbled a few words in his tribal language. The missionary
traveling with us interpreted that he said, "We walk from here."

We climbed out of the vehicle and began our trek. In the after-
noon sun, the heat was sweltering. Soon we came to a clearing,
and in the middle of nowhere sat a thatched hut all by itself. You

may have seen something like it in *National Geographic* or on the Discovery Channel.

As we approached, two children emerged from the hut. One was a twelve-year-old girl. The other was a ten-year-old boy. Their names were Mary and Abel. After we introduced ourselves, the two children began to tell us their story.

Mary and Abel had sent their younger sister, Palmira, to school for the day.

"Where are your parents?" we asked through the interpreter.

"We have no parents," Mary said. "We are Palmira's parents now."

In shock, we looked at one another. "What happened to your parents?" someone asked.

"They died of AIDS."

Those three children lived alone. It was like they were playing house, but it was definitely no game. It was everyday life for these three. Mary, twelve years of age, and Abel, ten years of age, were raising their five-year-old sister.

"How do you take care of yourselves?" I asked through the interpreter.

In a flash, Abel ran behind his hut. When he came back, he had a smile on his face and something in his hands. "I take these little reeds and weave them together to make mats," he said in his native language. It was obvious he was very proud of himself. "And then I take them to the market to sell them."

"What market?" I asked him through the translator. We had driven for miles and had seen no market. We hadn't seen much of anything, to be honest.

Abel pointed over his shoulder and said, "The market is that way."

The missionary told us going to the market was about a five-mile trip—one way. This boy made that trip twice a day . . . *by himself . . . on foot.*

Mary then took over the conversation and began to show us how she ground maize for the children to eat. She and her brother had a small area where they grew maize. She picked up a large pole that resembled a log and began to lift and drop it into a hollowed-out bowl, grinding the maize as she went. She looked at me and smiled and made a gesture I understood.

"You want me to try?" I asked.

She nodded.

I reached over and lifted the heavy log. I was amazed at its weight and her obvious strength. I raised and dropped the pole a few times, then stopped as I soon grew weary. This made Mary laugh.

As we stood there, the missionary shared with us how these children turned to prayer to survive. We heard more of their story and began to wrap up our visit.

"Can we share a song before you go?" Mary asked through the interpreter.

"Sure," our team responded.

As these two children began to sing to God, it was one of the most awesome sounds I had ever heard.

After the song, we began to pray. While we were praying, it was all I could do not to cry like a baby. God spoke to my heart and began to challenge me on what was important to me. He began to impress upon me, "What cause are you fighting for?"

Don't get me wrong. I don't feel guilty for being blessed to live in America. America affords us great freedoms. But I came to the realization that what is important for us might be a bit more authentic if it were purged through the challenges those in the third world face. People in other parts of the world who worship Jesus do not always have an easy road. They face many barriers and obstacles, and sometimes even death. (And those dangers may soon come to our country with the way things are going.)

My visit with Mary and Abel made me evaluate my priorities. Their "community" consisted of the three siblings.

When we gather in community, we learn something.

There are more important things than "me." There is a cause bigger than what most people are serving. That cause is the gospel.

Together Brings Focus

I remember going to pep rallies in high school on Friday afternoons. The school day would be cut short and we would get pumped up about the Friday night football game. Teachers and students united as we focused on defeating the crosstown rival. Acquaintances in the bleachers became best buddies as we directed all of our energy and attention toward defeating our common enemy: the opposing team. We had one goal, one cause we rallied around.

Habitat for Humanity is an organization that makes a huge difference in our world. Talk about rallying together around a cause. Many people think former president Jimmy Carter founded the organization. He didn't, but he has brought it widespread recognition.

The nonprofit organization traces its roots to Americus, Georgia, on Koinonia Farm (interesting name, right?), where farmer and scholar Clarence Jordan, along with Millard and Linda Fuller, began talking about "partnership housing"—those in need working alongside volunteers to build homes. The concept has grown to serve twenty-two million people and provide housing in seventy countries where Habitat provides stability and shelter by people working together.[1]

This happens every day in clubs and communities around the country too. A vision grows out of the richness of community and brings people together to serve.

The early church had that kind of vision. Acts 4 describes a powerful gathering where the people began to pray, and then the building began to shake.

After they prayed, the place where they were meeting was *shaken*. And they were all filled with the Holy Spirit. (Acts 4:31, emphasis added)

Talk about a pep rally! I'd love for that to happen today. I'm not sure if any of us would know how to respond. People in a community like this focus their attention and energy on one thing. It's not defeating a crosstown rival but defeating the enemy by worshiping Jesus . . . together. Worship provides the energy for believers to rally around a cause and serve Jesus.

Unfortunately, we've started to see worship as optional. And I understand why. Some of us have had negative experiences in worship. Perhaps we've seen worship services where the audience is the focus instead of God.

It reminds me of a story I heard from a worship pastor one time. He had someone come up to him at the end of the service.

"I didn't really like the worship songs we sang today," the consumer church member said.

"Did the songs contain anything that wasn't correct or was unbiblical or unsound?" the worship pastor asked.

"No, they just weren't songs I liked. The lyrics lifted God up and everything; I just didn't like them," she replied.

"Well, I didn't realize we were singing them to *you*," the pastor responded.

While that may sound harsh, he was right. Worshiping together provides the encouragement we need to pursue the disciplines that are essential to the faith. One reason so many believers don't grow in faith may be that they fail to worship in *community*.

Hebrews 10:24–25 reminds us to "stir up one another to love and good works, not neglecting to meet together, as is the habit of some, but encouraging one another, and all the more as you see the Day drawing near" (ESV).

Sometimes it's easy to blow off corporate worship because we didn't sleep well the night before, or we don't feel well, or we just don't have the time. Some people may even say, "I can worship by myself." Many believers justify this because of a bad church experience and feel like they have "been there, done that." Yet God did not make us to worship as solo individuals. Watching online worship services or listening to sermons is not adequate replacement for hearing God's Word preached in person alongside other believers in a local gathering of community. Please note, I'm not talking about a situation where an individual is unable to attend church. I'm talking about people who are able to go and choose not to.

Worship is essential in a community. I'm not talking about a going-through-the-motions service. Authentic worship is oftentimes the pep rally for believers to gather, find encouragement for the week, and give honor to God.

One of the wonderful benefits of not doing life alone is *the experience of authentic worship.* Worship is more than whatever "time" your church service occurs. Most of us have experienced a worship *service* where *worship* didn't happen. The early church was committed to wholehearted worship. From this early-church ragtag community of people, we learn what authentic worship is and what it is not.

Worship Is about the Heart

Worship, first and foremost, is a *heart* issue. We may sing certain songs and follow a predictable order in our times of worship. We may have some good traditions, but those don't take the place of authentic worship. And *authentic worship is experienced in community.*

A tradition can be an *act* of worship, but it can't *replace* worship. It's not about the methodology, but the message. Jesus hints at this in His explanation to the woman at the well when He says to her, "Woman, believe Me, an hour is coming when neither in this mountain nor in Jerusalem will you worship the Father" (John

4:21 NASB). Traditions are fine, but when they take the place of absolute truth, we have a problem.

For these early believers, worship was not confined to a place. Not a church, a beautiful beach, or a mountaintop. There are some people today whose worship is confined to a place, and I can promise you this: worship is not about being in a specific place.

A Real-Life Experience

When I was a youth pastor, our team was responsible for planning summer camp. It was my first summer at that church, and everyone just assumed we would go to the same camp they'd always gone to. I was a nineteen-year-old college freshman youth director. As the leadership and I began praying about where to go for summer camp, we felt God leading us somewhere different. I wasn't prepared for what was about to happen.

When we told the students, you would have thought we were taking them to the worst place on earth. All they could do was talk about how God showed up at the camp they went to every year, and if they did not go back there, God wouldn't show up. They would have the worst summer camp experience—ever.

I tried to explain that God could show up and work in any place, but they didn't believe me. However, I insisted. I knew they had something big to learn about God. Summer finally arrived, and after much reluctance and whining from the students—and prayer and determination from the leaders—we loaded up the van and headed off to camp, a long eight-hour van drive to Orlando, Florida.

It didn't take long for the students to realize they could meet with God anywhere. The worship times were incredible, and the speaker ministered to them in ways they really needed. The students met other young people from around the country with whom they never would have connected at the other camp. Relationships were made, and new faith friendships were created.

We had an amazing week of camp. God met us just as He promised He would, and the students were not only shocked but thankful.

They also learned an important lesson.

God is not confined to a place. God does not fit in a box. It was so incredible to see those students' eyes opened and to see them finally come to a heart understanding that we can experience God anywhere if we are open to seeing and hearing Him, and He can speak to anyone He chooses. The early church experienced authentic worship in various places *together*. They experienced it in the temple, in homes, inside, outside, in the morning, in the evening. There were no limitations for worship.

We may point fingers at the young people, but sometimes we adults are just as guilty about getting stuck in our ways. Sometimes those ways cause disconnection in our communities, and we need God to open our eyes to see it.

In our North American culture, *we give a lot of attention to the church being a place instead of it being a people.* "That [pointing to a building] is our church. That's not what the early church believed. They knew *they* were the church.

Real worship is all about heart transformation. In Acts 4:24, we read, "When they heard this, they raised their voices **together** in prayer to God. '*Sovereign Lord,*' they said, '*you made the heavens and the earth and the sea, and everything in them.*'" This proclamation came after Peter and John's report that the Sanhedrin had instructed them not to speak about Jesus anymore. Too late. Their hearts had been transformed by the gospel. Their 100 percent loyalty was with the Lord.

The experience of worship in community will help us to worship authentically, not just by moving our mouths to the words of the songs but by allowing those words to bring transformation to our lives. When our hearts have been changed, we'll never be just going through the motions.

We can't worship God if we don't know Him. And when we are growing in community, we begin to know Jesus more. The more we know Him, the more genuine our worship will become. The lives of others around us will sensitize our hearts to authentic worship. We won't be able to "fake it" in community.

The more you know God, the more you will want to be with Him.

In Psalm 133, King David describes how pleasing it is to God when His people dwell (abide, remain) together in unity. One way we can effectively dwell together in unity is to participate regularly in corporate worship gatherings. It's interesting to know that the origin of the word *corporate* means "body" or "form into a body."[2] There's something special that happens when the body of Christ comes together to set our attention and affections on Him, the one who loved us and gave Himself for us.

Although worship is not primarily about us, the benefits of this intentional act of corporate worship are priceless. King David describes unity as similar to scented oils or dew that flows from above, down to God's people. This description leads us to understand that God's anointing and blessing flows from His head, which is Jesus Christ, down to His body, which is us. When we worship God together as a body, the Holy Spirit finds this so attractive that He often increases our awareness of His presence, blesses His people with peace, and provides powerful direction and sensitivity for our lives.

It's crucial to our spiritual health that we move God's heart in these times of worship. Can you imagine how God feels when His children, His bride, come together in worship, declaring our love for Him? He's undone! It's vital to our spiritual health and well-being that we have an understanding that we move His heart, even in our weakness, with the simplest act of worship—the slightest glance from our eyes toward Him.

Experiencing authentic worship so satisfies our souls that we don't have to shop around for man-made substitutes. William Temple made this clear in his masterful definition of worship:

> For worship is the submission of all our nature to God. It is the quickening of conscience by His holiness; the nourishment of mind with His truth; the purifying of imagination by His beauty; the opening of the heart to His love; the surrender of will to His purpose—and all of this gathered up in adoration, the most selfless emotion of which our nature is capable and therefore the chief remedy for that self-centeredness which is our original sin and the source of all actual sin.[3]

Authentic worship is one of the wonderful benefits of not doing life alone.

A Lesson on Worship from Buffat Heights Church, Knoxville, Tennessee

I recently pinch-hit as a worship leader for a pastor friend of mine in Knoxville. The people of this church genuinely enjoyed worship. They were from various socioeconomic backgrounds and of different ages. But they had rallied themselves around worshiping God. I tried several things as the interim worship pastor to see how they would respond. I thought if I changed song styles or did something out of the box, someone would complain. I led worship with the choir; I led worship with their praise team. We had soloists. We had duets. We had choral songs. We had contemporary songs. We sang hymns.

No matter the song or style, everyone seemed to engage in worship. Now, keep in mind, only God knows our hearts, so only He knows if folks were genuinely worshiping. But it seemed to me they were. I was amazed. We have the impression that churches argue the most over worship music.

145

One Sunday I brought in a painter to lead us in worship through art. One week I pulled up a whiteboard, led the church in Laura Story's "Indescribable" (made well known by Chris Tomlin), and asked people to come up and write on the whiteboard one word that described God to them.

I was amazed at the reaction. The first ones out of their seats were the kindergarten-aged students who came up and wrote words such as *awesome, powerful, Creator, Savior*. Many were weeping before the service was over, including me. When people are gathered in community to focus on Christ, *they experience authentic worship*, and God does incredible things. I am grateful for friends at Buffat Heights for being sensitive to God's Spirit and truly desiring to worship God. Because of their focus, connection is happening among the congregation with one another and with God.

Benefits to Worshiping Together

Worshiping together is a powerful tool God has given us as believers. As I close this chapter, let me share quickly three benefits I have experienced with my worship community.

My faith has been energized. When I gather with others who have come to hear God's voice through singing, praying, and hearing God's Word, I am energized and encouraged to listen and grow. These worship gatherings are much like the pep rally we talked about earlier. These times give me fuel to go out and face life with my faith empowered. They remind me I am part of a family who is standing with me in worship of the one true God.

I connect personally with other people. I see their passion for God; I feel their hurts; I get to know their hearts as we worship together. Voices, eye contact, volume, intensity, expressions—all are part of worshiping together. I don't get this benefit by watching an online worship "experience." When I attend in real life, I see what moves people, and they see what moves me. My personal worship taste becomes less important as I see what enhances worship for those around me.

I grow. Spiritual fruit happens because I am connected with people in worship who can then hold me accountable to follow through on what we have heard, experienced, and been told by the Holy Spirit in worship. This dynamic moves me from being a hearer of the Word to becoming a doer of the Word and growing as a disciple.

Our corporate/community worship times help us build one another up as well as praise God for His greatness. It's such corporate synergy of us worshiping together that serves as fuel in the engine for the body of Christ to do what God has called us to do. Flashback: think about the early church in Acts. Do you think they needed that synergy? Did they need that Spirit-induced power from worshiping together? I think so. Do we need that power in our lives today? I know so. This is just another way we are better together.

Are you ready to rally around a cause with others? Do you long for a group of friends who have something in common? When you combine forces with others for a like cause, the results will be more than you ever imagined. And that's the "better together" story of my friend Mike Williams I'll share in the next chapter.

PRACTICAL QUESTIONS TO CONSIDER

1. How does your faith community keep its focus on God?

_____

_____

_____

2. What can happen if people focus more on the things that accompany worship than who they are to worship?

_____

_____

_____

3. What things have you experienced in worship with your community?

_____

_____

_____

4. How has worshiping with other people transformed your faith?

_____

_____

_____

PUT IT INTO PRACTICE

Attend the next worship service at your church or find and visit a special worship service in your area.

Watch as people worship, and sense what people around you are experiencing. What things do you see? What observations can you make? How does worship seem to impact individuals and the group as a whole?

CHAPTER FOURTEEN

Together, We Can

Talent wins games, but teamwork and intelligence win championships.

Michael Jordan

The call came almost ten years ago from my friend Mike. A comedian by trade, Mike used to kick off the weeks of summer youth camps our ministry led back in the nineties. Many years had passed since that last youth camp, but I still kept up with Mike through newsletters and other pastor friends. One day my phone rang. "Why don't you come down to the Dominican Republic and see what we are doing?" Mike politely asked. I kindly told Mike I was too busy, and he just as kindly said, "I understand." But a few weeks later my phone rang again, and we had the same conversation.

The word *relentless* describes Mike when he's committed to something.

After about the fourth call, I finally agreed, and we settled on a date for me to go down to the Dominican Republic to see the work of the mission Mike piloted. Not wanting to go alone, I asked my family, of course, and mentioned to some friends online that I was going. The next thing I knew, we had sixteen volunteers ready to go down and serve. Volunteers were quickly recruited, by the way, because we were connected in community. When we arrived, Mike and his team met us, and we began our week together. Over the course of our time together on the ground, Mike shared his story with me.

I was never able to get that first trip down to the Dominican Republic out of my mind. Trust me, I tried. Why would God want me here? I would *not* make a good missionary. I'm a comedian. My spiritual gift is sarcasm. I am well versed to stand up in front of crowds and make them laugh for ninety minutes and go home. I don't think I can help people laugh their hunger away. If laughter could satisfy hunger, I would not be fat. Another reason I asked why God would want me here—I was making a real nice living telling these jokes.

For a while, I squelched the call by raising a lot of money for the mission. I convinced myself that was the best of both worlds. However, the yearning inside kept pulling me to a boots-on-the-ground position. I have come to learn that God does not need my money, nor does He need my boots on the ground. But I need to be doing what He wants me to do when He wants me to do it.

A few months later my wife and I put our house on the market, had a big garage sale, packed our bags, and moved to the Dominican Republic, the most human-trafficked country in the western hemisphere and one of the most corrupt governments in the free world. So, it seemed like a great idea to raise our four children there. Um . . . not at all. But when God calls you to go somewhere—across the world or across the street—you have a choice. What will you do? Let's be honest. Safety anywhere is just a dream. If you don't believe me, please watch the news tonight.

I remember the day we landed at that little airport with twelve suitcases, six backpacks, and a guitar. We had no financial support. We were following a New Testament style of mission funding made popular by the apostle Paul called tent-making. To support his mission work, Paul made tents and sold them. I have no idea how big they were. Maybe they were pup tents, family tents, or circus tents, for that matter. I don't know. I do know that he was willing to put in his own sweat equity to do what God had called him to do. We had chosen to do the same. Using the time many missionaries would come home on furlough, I would come home and tell jokes to raise our support.

We had little idea of what God wanted us to accomplish. Had I known the large scale of His plan, I would have most likely chickened out. My visions are usually much smaller than His designs. I build birdhouses. God creates trees and then forests. Today we operate a mission that serves hundreds of people. We serve a poor, rural mountain-top area where the children are the targets of sex traffickers. We're trying to rescue a whole lot of girls from certain destruction.

Among the poor here is a tragic fairy tale. Here's how the story goes: a young teenage girl goes to town and meets a foreign man. She pleases him in every way he asks. He comes to visit her again and again. One day this foreign man takes her back to America or Germany or Spain, and the girl lives happily ever after in a big, fancy house. Now, because she is rich, she can send money back to her very poor family and her brothers and sisters can have a better life.

How tragic is this lie? How many young girls fall into this fairy tale trap and end up the discards of the perverts that visit our shores? Our mission programs empower young girls to make choices for success that don't include selling themselves.

We also have the joy of bringing relief to the Haitian refugees living in the dump. These poorest of the poor lost their homes during an earthquake. Now they live in squalor. What can a Jesus follower do? Through the small gifts of people working together in the United States, we have an ongoing feeding ministry program bringing hot soup, peanut butter sandwiches, and cold, clean water to those people. It has been our joy to serve these dear humble people, as many of them call Jesus Christ their Savior and Lord.

God has allowed us to build houses and bridges. We have been able to touch the lives of deaf children and bring glasses to those whose eyes were becoming blind in old age. We have helped start businesses for widows and install roofs for families. We have been able to join God on some of the greatest adventures you could imagine.

Sure, there have been hurts along the way. Some days we weep. I can tell you of a girl whose mother has been selling her to a neighbor since she was eight years old. How did this slip past us? Now she is pregnant, and the school doesn't allow pregnant girls to attend. What do I say to her? We hold her hand and promise to be there from now on.

I think of another young lady. An old padlock secures her young child behind a wooden door of their single-room shack as this young mother heads out to find someone who will buy her for enough food to feed her and her child. You can look the other way when you don't know their name, but when you know their name, it's not so easy. She brings her child to our Bible programs. She sits with the children and tries to live the childhood she never received.

There are days that the work seems so big and impossible that it brings us to tears, but we get up the next morning ready to charge the gates of hell again. Why? Because we have chosen to join God in making a difference, not just making a statement. And hundreds of people around the world who have joined our cause are making this happen every day.

The Crossover CUPS Mission is blessed to be accomplishing so much because of one very important reason. People have realized they are better together. Because this was part of the culture Mike created at the beginning, there is no one person, corporation, or grant-making entity that helps the mission accomplish its vision. It is hundreds of people cooperating together for one cause: the cause of Christ. It is people who are connected to God and to one another in community who are moving mountains.

We are better together. It is astounding what can be done when we work together. But maybe you don't see it yet in your community or in your church. What will it take to get there? Let's talk about that next.

PRACTICAL QUESTIONS TO CONSIDER

1. What dream has God given you? If you're not sure, you can ask Him for one.

2. What cause do you believe in? What could happen if people worked together to accomplish the mission of that cause?

3. What cause is God calling you to?

PUT IT INTO PRACTICE

Find a cause in your community you believe in, and get behind it with your time, talent, or treasure. Reach out to some of the people who support that cause and begin to dialogue about what drives their passion for it.

CHAPTER FIFTEEN

What Will It Take?

> In life, you have three choices: give up, give in, or give
> it your all.
>
> Unknown

I'm getting to that age. It's known as old. It was time for
another eye exam. I kept telling my wife I was seeing water
buffalo in the roads at night. She would laugh at me and
say, "You need to get some new glasses." She was right. I had
put it off as long as I could. When you can't see clearly, glasses
or contacts are lifesavers, bringing objects back into focus—
and allowing you to avoid the buffalo in the middle of the
road.

Unity serves as the corrective lens we need to do community
and life together. Unity brings focus. We read in Acts 4:32 that
"all the believers were **united** in heart and mind" (NLT, emphasis
added). They were united around a common "thing." They shared

something similar. For them it was their relationship with Jesus and their desire to follow His teachings as disciples. That pursuit connected them in community. That goal helped them stay focused. That common relationship with Jesus was the driving force for everything they did.

And guess what? This is our answer to real community as well. Jesus Christ is the ultimate example of one who lived a life not characterized by self-centeredness but by selflessness. He emptied Himself so we could be filled. He knew all along that none of us would be truly self-sufficient, so He became the *sufficient sacrifice* on our behalf when He died on the cross. He did this so we wouldn't have to. The Christian life is not one of independence and autonomy but rather dependence upon the God of the universe. It is my hope and prayer that we can each *give our all* to this idea of **being better together**. Being better together can be a powerful solution for loneliness.

> Although He existed in the form of God, [Jesus] did not regard equality with God a thing to be grasped, but emptied Himself, taking the form of a bond-servant, and being made in the likeness of men. (Phil. 2:6–7 NASB)

How can we begin to move toward the kind of community to which God is calling us? What are some simple steps to help us?

Recreate "Old School" Friendships

When I was seven years old, I lived on Sunline Place. What a great name for a street! My friend lived next door, and we used to spend every moment we could together. We rode our Big Wheels up and down the street, swam at the neighbor's pool, and helped direct the neighborhood talent shows. It was hard to get us to come inside before dark because we wanted to take advantage of every moment of daylight to play, make memories, and have a good time.

Today we play online games with people we can't see. I used to have to go next door and ask, "Can Tommy come out and play?" But now, our "friendships" are virtual. We don't even have to see the "friend" with whom we are playing. Scary . . . and dangerous too.

My challenge to you (and myself) is to recreate some "old school" friendships. I'm not suggesting you pull out your old high school or college yearbook and reach out to long-lost people you haven't talked to in ten, twenty, or thirty years. I'm suggesting you create the kinds of friendships you had back then with the people who are in your life at this moment.

When you have conversations in person, things happen that just can't happen in a virtual setting. It's too easy to be passive in virtual conversations. It's also very easy to multitask. Even while I'm writing this book, my instant messenger is "dinging" behind the manuscript, causing me to stop every few minutes and reply to someone. They have no idea what I am doing while I am carrying on a conversation with them.

So, pick up the phone and call a friend. Go see them. Do something together that requires more than sitting and watching a screen (we can do this alone). Eat a meal with them. Have a conversation. Let's go back to that "old school" type of friendship. Sounds fun, doesn't it?

Maybe you have seen the Nissan commercial where a guy receives a text from a friend. Instead of answering the text, he jumps in his new Nissan and drives to his friend's house. When his friend opens the door, he says, "Not much, how about you?" His friend smiles and says, "Are you answering my text in person?"[1] That's the kind of "old school" type of friendship recreating I am talking about.

However, to do that, we may also have to change our thinking.

Recalibrating Our Thinking

Incredible things can be accomplished when we do life together. But for some of us, we may need a new way of thinking. Perhaps that's the *greatest* challenge—changing our mindset. We change what we do by changing what we think. What we believe controls how we behave. You've read stories here of believers doing fantastic work that required rethinking how to do life, how to impact people. Change didn't come easy. At First Baptist, Leesburg, people had to be willing to meet the social ills facing the community around them. In the Dominican Republic, remarkable things have happened and are *still* happening in Mike's work as a result of changed thinking. The fruit of each of these groups came from realizing that *we are better together.*

According to *Merriam-Webster's Dictionary*, to calibrate means "to standardize . . . by determining the deviation from a standard so as to ascertain the proper correction."[2]

Recalibrating our thinking is a big step toward doing life together. God has a plan for our lives that includes being together in person. When we calibrate our minds to His plan, we can evaluate how closely our lives match His plan. Sometimes we have to allow God to adjust our thinking:

> Therefore, I urge you, brothers and sisters, in view of God's mercy, to offer your bodies as a living sacrifice, holy and pleasing to God— this is your true and proper worship. Do not conform to the pattern of this world, but be transformed by the renewing of your mind. Then you will be able to test and approve what God's will is—his good, pleasing and perfect will. (Rom. 12:1–2)

Megan Paraiso, a young wife and mom, explained it this way on the Wave Church blog:

> Relationships at one point meant only hanging out when it was convenient for me or if I had nothing better to do. I could occupy

myself just fine or hang out with my family and I was content. I would get a phone call almost every weekend from my grade school bestie wanting to get together, and 90% of the time, I'd turn her down. I honestly don't know how I kept her around all these years; but thank God she stuck it out! I was an introverted homebody. I placed little value on relationships. I did not want to be self-centered—I was just oblivious to the fact that I was self-centered.[3]

Megan's honesty reveals the attitude of a lot of us. She confesses that most of the time, she was thinking only of herself. And while it's fine to think of ourselves from time to time, for the most part, we need to shift our focus outward. To start thinking *we instead of me,* we may need some recalibration.

Re-Member, Not Dismember

A few weeks ago, my wife and I were going through the mail. Bill, bill, newsletter, bill, advertisement, bill, bill. One bill was our automobile insurance. I wasn't too excited about opening that one since our two children are both still under twenty-five, but I did. Have you ever read the small print on your auto insurance? Especially on the coverage areas? This is from our insurance:

> AD&D insurance covers exactly what its name states: accidental death and dismemberment. What does this mean? In the event of a fatal accident or an accident that results in you losing your eyesight, speech, hearing, or a limb, AD&D will pay you or your beneficiaries a specified amount. However, there are restrictions and exclusions. To receive benefits related to an accident, your injuries or death usually must occur within a few months of the accident date. Also, you will only collect benefits if your death or injuries are proven, direct results of the accident.

Now, there's a happy thought. Losing your eye or a limb. It made me queasy, and I wanted to think about something else. Losing a limb—being *dismembered*—is a gruesome thought. However, Pastor Greg Boyd suggests this is a great image to help us understand the importance of the body of Christ.[4]

Think about how important every part, every member of the body of Christ, is to the health of the community. Then think about what it means for the body to be dismembered. Paul puts it this way:

> For just as the body is one and has many members, and all the members of the body, though many, are one body, so it is with Christ. For in one Spirit we were all baptized into one body—Jews or Greeks, slaves or free—and all were made to drink of one Spirit.
>
> For the body does not consist of one member but of many. If the foot should say, "Because I am not a hand, I do not belong to the body," that would not make it any less a part of the body. And if the ear should say, "Because I am not an eye, I do not belong to the body," that would not make it any less a part of the body. (1 Cor. 12:12–16 ESV)

Our bodies constantly work to function as the healthiest versions of ourselves. The slightest disruption, sickness, or injury can cause health issues that move our bodies into "repair mode."

The good news is God, our Father, is also our Great Physician. It's interesting to consider that God often refers to His people as "the body of Christ" and has given us some great instruction through His Word on how to properly care for the body—His people, His prized possession. Because He created us, He knows exactly what it takes to keep His body healthy and in proper balance. Just like the human body, the body of Christ is meant to function as a whole—not independently from its other parts. It's necessary and beneficial to our spiritual health and well-being that His body functions together in unity.

159

I often hear people say, "I can worship by myself" or "I don't need the group at the church; I can get to know God on my own." Even if this were true—and it's really not—it misses the value of the body of Christ that is crucial to living as a believer. You may be a part of the body the rest of us need. And without you, the body will be incomplete. You have something to contribute to the body that will help it function as God intended.

We belong to one another. We function best when we work together. We don't have to follow Christ solo—nor should we. Interdependence, not independence, is God's plan for His children. When we fail to connect and do life with each other, we are failing to connect with Jesus.

> For as in one body we have many members, and the members do not all have the same function, so we, though many, are one body in Christ, and individually members one of another. (Rom. 12:4–5 ESV)

There are those, even in Christian circles, who would try to dissuade me from believing this type of togetherness is possible. And yet, Paul talks about Jesus dying for this kind of community.

> Therefore be imitators of God, as beloved children. And walk in love, as Christ loved us and gave himself up for us, a fragrant offering and sacrifice to God. (Eph. 5:1–2 ESV)

Would He give His life for something we couldn't do in the twenty-first century? I don't think so. The New Testament tells story after story about communities that experienced so much togetherness it would be hard to imagine believers dealing with loneliness. Christ has called us to love and serve one another. We may just have to be willing to think outside the box and do something different. Our culture has programmed us to do life in a way that directly contradicts how the Bible instructs believers to live. We can change that.

Our lives once centered around family. I remember hearing stories of multiple generations living under one roof or in close proximity to one another. Now we value individualism and rely on ourselves. We brag about being independent, and many of us live far away from where we were raised. If we have time for connections at all, they're work connections that are usually shallow and short-lived.

As believers, we have the great freedom and privilege to enjoy living in community and being better together with our spiritual families. We don't have to do life alone. We can experience the joy of having close relationships. We don't have to *settle* for being part of a community because there's nothing better. We have the privilege of relying on the body when we are struggling or in need. There is nothing better than that.

It is, indeed, countercultural. Individualism and doing life on our own seem to be the norm. But this way of living is far from God's best plan for us. God's plan is community. The evidence is there from the beginning. After creating the world, God gave Adam a helpmate (Gen. 2:18) because He did not want man to be alone. But it didn't stop there.

God chose the Israelites to be His people: "And I will walk among you and will be your God, and you shall be my people" (Lev. 26:12 ESV). They lived and worshiped Him together in community. Following His death and resurrection, Christ ordained and instituted the next level of community: "Now you are the body of Christ and individually members of it" (1 Cor. 12:27 ESV).

We call it the church.

Paul Tripp says in his book *Whiter Than Snow: Meditations on Sin and Mercy,*

> We weren't created to be independent, autonomous, or self-sufficient. We were made to live in a humble, worshipful, and loving dependency upon God and in a loving and humble

interdependency with others. Our lives were designed to be community projects. Yet, the foolishness of sin tells us that we have
all that we need within ourselves. So, we settle for relationships
that never go beneath the casual. We defend ourselves when the
people around us point out a weakness or a wrong. We hold our
struggles within, not taking advantage of the resources God has
given us.[5]

I so appreciate the caution Tripp gives: "not taking advantage
of the resources God has given us." God knew life would be difficult in this world, so He providentially created the concept of
community to be a way to strengthen us. Unfortunately, we often
fail to take advantage of it.

Even though superficiality is a disease of our time, we don't
have to live this way. Shallow friendships and fragile relationships
mark our society, but they don't have to mark us. Because believers of Jesus follow a different path than the rest of the world, the
way we live and the way we connect with one another should be
drastically different. It's a journey meant to be traveled together.
Coming together in Christ can show the world that Jesus is Lord.
We are living in a time when the world needs to see this more
than ever.

People will be more persuaded by the lives our faith produces
than by the belief system we champion. Sometimes we want people
to just accept our beliefs and make them their own. They will never
be interested in making them their own until they see those beliefs
create a change in us. Truly, changed lives will persuade others. The
early church's consistent daily lifestyle and visible transformation
silenced those who wanted to belittle and degrade it. The truth of
Christ is both validated and vindicated when we are the members
of the body living life together. How exciting that we get to be the
people to model this to the world! What a great benefit of doing
life with others!

My prayer is that discovering the benefits of genuine "old school" friendship and community will give you the boldness and courage to seek these kinds of relationships more often. Friendships like this have enabled me to steadily plod through the life to which God has called me. God has given us this gift of friendship and community for a reason. And though these genuine friendships are not always easy to find, I've realized that the challenge of finding them has made me appreciate them even more.

PRACTICAL QUESTIONS TO CONSIDER

1. How do you feel you are living your life? Are you living more solo Christianity or Christianity in community?

2. What challenges do you see for us as believers when it comes to trying to live in real community?

3. What negative effects have you seen in the lives of people who are living life alone, spiritually speaking?

4. What does God need to recalibrate in your mind to help you see doing life with others the way He sees it?

5. Does it bother you to think about how the body of Christ is sometimes dismembered? Or are you connected and aware that you are part of the body of Christ? How can you tell?

6. What do you need to do to experience the kind of community God has for you? Are you willing to do it?

PUT IT INTO PRACTICE

If you want to read more about community and real friendships, the next two chapters are for those who passionately and desperately desire for the body of Christ to accurately reflect what Christ intended and connect with more people in an ever-disconnected, or overconnected, world.

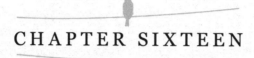

CHAPTER SIXTEEN

You Gotta Have Faith

A Letter to Christ Followers

The True Church can never fail. For it is based upon
a rock.

T. S. Eliot

I wanted to end this book with two letters. One of the letters is to those of us who call ourselves Christ followers, who are part of the church. The church is not a building. The church is a people. The church is more than those who attend *your* local church each week.

The letter in the *next chapter* is to those in places of leadership. Believers and their leaders will need to work together to ensure real connection happens in a world dealing with sensory overload. Maybe it's a world that is *overconnected.*

Dear Christ followers,

One of the greatest struggles we face, especially if we live in the Bible Belt, is realizing God is bigger than our local faith community, our local church. He is bigger than any one single church. God is even bigger than all the churches in the country. God is the God of the universe, of all creation, and He is Lord of every group that gathers in His name. The reason this perspective is important is because it plays a major role in defining how we see church and thus, how we see working together . . . with other believers. If we miss this perspective, we may unknowingly turn our focus inward and make people feel lonely.

As I was writing this book, I had in mind the many faces of friends who have pulled away from community, and especially their faith community, because they tried to find connection but failed. Some of us might have experienced this same kind of challenge in a physical sense when we were young and playing the game red rover. We ran hard to the other side and tried to break through the chain of people, but we couldn't break through. Many individuals I have talked to who have experienced loneliness share this experience of being unable to connect with others.

If God is to reach your city, He is probably going to need every believer to do so. (And He may choose to use unbelievers and the ungodly to accomplish His agenda. Just take a look at our world now.) And because every believer doesn't go to the same local church—every believer is not part of the same local body—He is going to need every Bible-believing church body to accomplish His goal. How often have you thought about that? How often do churches in cities work together? Let's be honest: believers, and many times churches, work against one another. Sometimes this happens because of insecurity, and sometimes it is because we mistakenly think our local body of believers is superior to another. And even if we acknowledge that our local church is not better, what are we doing to express we believe this?

Thankfully, in most cities, churches aren't working against other churches. But they can be working parallel to one another. This is better but still lacks the depth of gospel impact Paul describes in Ephesians 2:11–22:

> Therefore, remember that formerly you who are Gentiles by birth and called "uncircumcised" by those who call themselves "the circumcision" (which is done in the body by human hands)—remember that at that time you were separate from Christ, excluded from citizenship in Israel and foreigners to the covenants of the promise, without hope and without God in the world. But now in Christ Jesus you who once were far away have been brought near by the blood of Christ.
>
> For he himself is our peace, who has made the two groups one and has destroyed the barrier, the dividing wall of hostility, by setting aside in his flesh the law with its commands and regulations. His purpose was to create in himself one new humanity out of the two, thus making peace, and in one body to reconcile both of them to God through the cross, by which he put to death their hostility. He came and preached peace to you who were far away and peace to those who were near. For through him we both have access to the Father by one Spirit.
>
> Consequently, you are no longer foreigners and strangers, but fellow citizens with God's people and also members of his household, built on the foundation of the apostles and prophets, with Christ Jesus himself as the chief cornerstone. In him the whole building is joined together and rises to become a holy temple in the Lord. And in him you too are being built together to become a dwelling in which God lives by his Spirit.

Paul suggests each individual person is part of the local body of believers. And each individual body of believers is part of the body of believers all over the globe. Many people work on the same goals, but most people do so without working together. When we do this separately from one another, it "just leads to isolation and breeds apathy for one another's work."[1]

Working together as a group of believers from various churches and denominations requires intentionality. Most churches focus on the vision for their individual ministry or church, and understandably so. Getting consensus on a church's vision is sometimes a monumental task. But when we understand our vision for our church is only part of God's plan for our community or city, it compels us to work toward a bigger vision, allowing us to combine our resources with those of other churches in order to have a gospel vision. As Kelly Seely says, "A win-win situation is achieved when autonomous [local] groups of believers realize they need one another—not only for their own benefit but also to fulfill the Great Commission."[2]

This all sounds well and good, but is it really just pie-in-the-sky thinking? How can we pull this off when churches deal with territorialism and egos? When we are approached to think about something "out of the box," do we ask, "How will this benefit us or our church?" or "Will this build our recognition in the community?" instead of asking, "Does this advance God's kingdom?"

Sometimes the fear is that if we work together with other churches, some people may decide to move to another local body because they have more resources than our own. If that fear sounds like more of a controlling attitude, it is. But that's not our goal as members of the body. Our church should be equipping us and then unleashing us to do the ministry ourselves that each one of us has been gifted to do. It's this attitude of controlling instead of releasing and unleashing that sets up your church and mine to be more consumer driven. We start to cater to what people want instead of challenging people to be who God needs.

So, what are some things we can do to encourage our faith community that will address and perhaps even defeat the pain of loneliness?

First, seek out a gospel-believing local church. If you have already found one, help those in your circle of influence see your local body of believers as a piece of the puzzle, not the whole puzzle.

Second, encourage your pastor to think this way. Most pastors want to think this way, but because of the pressure of a consumeristic society (and even some in the local church), they settle for accomplishing the vision of their own local church. This is an important calling, but as I have said, it falls short of the full vision to which God has called each one of us.

Third, remember the reasons to work together as groups of believers, the most obvious of which is the ability to reach more people. We can accomplish more together.

Working together can change the perception of community. People sometimes think local churches are more concerned about taking care of our own than others in the community. Why? Because they rarely see churches working together for the cause of Christ. What an opportunity we have to impact our communities and show the love of Christ by working outside the walls of our church and working with other faith communities!

These are just a few ideas to help us connect with other faith communities, thereby fighting the pain of loneliness. I am praying for you.

Striving for real connection,
Jack

PRACTICAL QUESTIONS TO CONSIDER

1. How has God spoken to you about working together? What mindset, if any, does God need to change in your church to allow you to partner with other local bodies of believers in the community?

2. What steps can you take personally in your faith community when opportunities arise to work together?

3. How can you pray specifically for those next steps?

PUT IT INTO PRACTICE

Take time to write a letter or email to an area pastor or ministry leader and encourage them in their work. Let them know you are thankful for what they are doing to make a positive impact in the community.

CHAPTER SEVENTEEN

Encouraging Leaders Who Are Lonely

A Letter to Leaders

If you know a leader who is lonely, please encourage him/her to reach out to someone. If they don't have someone with whom they can talk, share my name.

Jack Eason

I sat there sipping on hot chocolate and working on my laptop. The clatter of dishes echoed just behind me in the coffee shop, but I could make out some of the conversation happening next to me.

"Well, I think it's time for him to go, he's been here long enough," said one lady.

Another lady chimed in. "Yes, and he seems to be so unconcerned with us. He never comes to visit our group and make us feel important."

171

"Maybe we can start a petition and have him voted out," the older gentleman added as he placed his coffee cup beside the Bible on their table.

"Let's just pray that happens soon," the first lady responded.

I tried to keep my cool, because I had picked up enough of the conversation to know what they were talking about. What grieved me, without knowing any details of the situation, was that none of them talked about praying *for* the pastor, or even checking on him. It was just a lot of complaining.

We began this book by talking about loneliness, mentioning the elderly and millennials, but other people who came to mind were my friends in ministry. Pastors and ministry leaders can be some of the loneliest people on the planet because they are always serving and rarely have someone to listen and minister to them.

I wanted to add this final short chapter to this book for many reasons. First, I hope that every person reading this will take the opportunity, for just a moment, to put themselves in their pastor's shoes. Maybe you have left a faith community because your pastor or another ministry leader dropped the ball, made a mistake, or didn't do what was expected. I understand. It happens. I'm not making excuses for him or her, condoning any wrong behavior, or trying to explain away anything that happened that may have resulted in you not seeing the Jesus of the Bible.

For some reason, we forget that those God has called to lead us in our faith communities are not superhuman, nor are they super-Christian. They're men and women, prone to sin, but striving to honor God. Just like us. And sometimes they fail way more than they'd like to admit. While there are some egregious acts happening among leaders in the church—for which there is no excuse—most pastors I know want to serve their people and honor God with their lives.

"More than half of evangelical and Reformed pastors told the Schaeffer Institute in 2015 and 2016 that although they're happier than they were the previous year (79 percent), they don't have any good and true friends (58 percent). About the same number reported they can't meet their church's unrealistic expectations (52 percent)."[1] It's a challenging occupation and calling to be sure. Ministry leaders are hard on themselves as well, "often judging themselves for sins of omission and commission," Chuck Hannaford said.[2] Chuck is a clinical psychologist who works with many pastors. Oftentimes, pastors and ministry leaders are isolated because they don't really have anyone with whom they can be transparent. They feel if they are too transparent with anyone in their congregation that they may be seen as failures.

Serving as a pastor requires self-sacrifice, putting the needs of the congregation first and expending time and energy—often getting nothing in return.[3] So, I just want to say this: your pastor needs encouragement. Your pastor needs grace. Your pastor needs support.

Pastors and ministry leaders tend to spiritualize solitude. And rightly so in some instances. Spending time alone with God *is* part of the process of growing spiritually. But every pastor and ministry leader know it's exactly that. *Part* of the equation.[4]

God has created all of us for community. When pastors neglect this important facet in their lives, then it's not a good thing.[5] "While pastors are learning how to include other leaders in vision and preaching, which is important, and pastors are also releasing power and responsibility to other leaders so that others help to carry the load, which is also good, the reality is, the pastor still carries much of the weight of the church. The pastor and his family are often the ones attacked by those in the church, outside the church and Satan."[6]

Sometimes, Satan's tactic is to make us think our church is the only one that can make community impact. When I was a church planter, I took a training series about reaching culture and working with other churches. When we entered the auditorium for our first session, the leader of the training began with the question, "If God brought revival to your community through the body of believers at the church up the street, would you be happy or jealous?" The room was quiet. It was a hard question, because most church leaders work diligently to accomplish goals for their local body; they forget there's a bigger picture. And that bigger picture is the entirety of the body of Christ, His bride, being used for His glory.

In fact, this "disguised solitude" often results in more loneliness, which, if ignored, will lead to depression. And when depression happens, things will only get worse. Most ministry leaders I know run at such a rapid pace with little downtime that many of them never realize they're lonely—until they stop. Then it all comes crashing in on them. As we've said, being around people doesn't equate to not being alone or lonely. And once depression hits, the next step is burnout.[7] Often when people are burned out, they are more tempted to fall into things—that is, sin—that can take them out of ministry. If you're a ministry leader who is feeling lonely, please reach out. If you know a leader who is feeling lonely, please reach out to him or her. Or maybe print out the letter below and send it to him or her. You can replace "Ministry Leader" with your leader's name and sign your name at the end.

Carey Nieuwhof offers some suggestions for ministry leaders that can help them avoid being lonely.[8] I want to share them below as a letter from me to you if you are a ministry leader. (I want to encourage you to share these tips with your pastor or ministry leader if you are a layperson.)

Dear Ministry Leader,

First of all, thank you for your commitment to serving people. I understand the sacrifice you are making. I also know that many times you may feel that no one understands and find yourself feeling lonely. When you feel this way, please, please do something about it.

It's easy to find yourself alone because of your position and leadership. Solitude can be good. But isolation is of the enemy. In fact, I encourage you to schedule time with your family and friends so you can engage with people.

Also, please cultivate relationships with others so that when you do feel lonely, you have someone to call. Cultivating relationships takes time. I have spent the better part of three decades building and nurturing relationships with numerous people, and I have less than a dozen that I can call at any time of day or night. That's the challenge of real relationships, but it's worth taking the time to create and cultivate them. As a ministry leader, I encourage you to make that a priority when it comes to how you map out your time. The people you're building these relationships with don't have to be part of your local church, and sometimes it is better if they aren't. Some of the relationships can even be outside your city. My close connections often operate similar organizations, love me for who I am, and understand the pressures that leaders face. They also know when I'm faking it or going through the motions and will call me out on it.

Before you think you don't need relationships within your church, let me encourage you to consider creating a few strong relationships with those inside your ministry. Having friends outside your organization is one thing, but you also need great friends inside your organization or church.

If you're a ministry leader and you're struggling with loneliness, I implore you to take the risk and reach out to someone. I want you to know that I love and genuinely care about you more than you will ever know. When I think about you, this Scripture comes to mind: "Regard them very highly in love because of their work" (1 Thess. 5:13 HCSB).

Praying for you today,
Jack

I pray if you know someone who needs to hear those words, that you will share the letter or write one of your own to them.

PRACTICAL QUESTIONS TO CONSIDER

1. How can you pray specifically for your pastor or ministry leader and the issue of loneliness?

_____

_____

2. If you are a pastor or ministry leader, do you have some friends you can confide in when it comes to the issue of loneliness?

_____

_____

3. What steps can you take to protect yourself against loneliness?

_____

_____

PUT IT INTO PRACTICE

Take a moment to text, email, or call your pastor or ministry leader. Schedule a time to meet with them in person. Offer to take them out to eat or just to connect, in real life, and encourage them. Take time to pray with them while you are together. Let them know that you are there for them.

CHAPTER EIGHTEEN

Final Words

Before we wrap up, let me share another story of a faith community working together and making an impact in Minnesota because their pastor was encouraged with his vision.

There aren't a lot of places for small children to play in the small town of Northfield, Minnesota, especially during the cold and snowy winter months. No one wants to go outside when the temperature is in negative digits. So the pastor urged the people of Northfield United Methodist Church to do something about it. The group purchased toys for area children, filled up their gym, and opened it up to the community. Twice a week, young children and their parents or caregivers are invited to "stop by for playtime. . . . The church's carpeted gym is stocked with trikes, slides, tunnels, basketball hoops, balls,"[1] and more things that kids enjoy.

Rev. Jerad Morey estimates that forty to fifty families from the community come by for these scheduled playtimes, most of whom are not part of the church. And that's perfectly all right with him. The people of Northfield UMC have "also been intentional about

following up with the families that come to playtime by collect-
ing their email addresses and then inviting them to other church
events—like a movie night"[2]—for the sole purpose of meeting the
needs of the people.

> "When describing what the holy city will look like when God is
> living in it, the prophet Zechariah says, 'the streets of the city
> shall be full of boys and girls playing in its streets,'" said Morey.
> "Northfield doesn't want 3-year-olds running down its city streets
> in January, but we do feel closer to heaven when we're in a room
> full of children's smiles and laughter."[3]

This is the power of working together. This is what happens
when biblical community, the church, is operating as it should.
We find meaningful connections despite the disconnected world
in which we live.

The Greatness of the Church

I believe in my heart that stories like Jerad's happen every day in
churches around the country and around the world. There is no
community like the church. Yes, we have our issues. I've admitted
those throughout this book. And I am okay with them. In fact,
it may be the imperfection that causes us to sharpen one another
and help one another grow.

How I love believers gathered together in community! I have
deep friendships with fellow believers that have lasted throughout
my lifetime. I have experienced my own needs being met by others
in my faith community. Many times, I have had the joy of meeting needs myself. There is a level of trust and vulnerability with
several of my church friends that I can't find anywhere else on the
planet. This transparency and accountability have propelled me
in my faith in ways I can't begin to express.

There truly is something unexplainable about the fellowship found in the church. The coming together of God's people giving Him praise is unmistakable. To experience the prayer of another believer for the needs of someone you love can't be matched by any other form of communication. This is the church. This is God's solution to loneliness: community. Even God Himself did not want to be alone so He created man in His image and then woman. Community, God's idea, is the solution for loneliness.

If you have a faith community that you are plugged into, I hope this encourages you to dig deeper and plant yourself there. I hope what you have read encourages you to pray for your pastors and leadership and to invest yourself where God has placed you. My prayer is that you will be an instrument, a part of the body, in that local fellowship to help people experience connectedness and love. By doing this, you will help people who might feel lonely to instead find a place of belonging and hope. Enjoy the benefits of being connected in a faith community: love, trust, authenticity, accountability, prayer, worship, and faith. There are so many blessings God has given to us when we invest in a connected community! Will you dig deeper? Will you not just dip your toe in the shallow end of the faith community but dive into the deep end of church?

If you aren't yet plugged into a church or you are still looking for one, I hope this book encourages you to consider the benefits of meaningful connection that can happen in a church family. My prayer is that you will find a church community to whom you can commit and that you would invest your time in that community. I know that you have gifts, talents, and life experience from which a church family could benefit. Until you find them, they will be missing a piece of their body, so I pray that you will diligently seek them out because they are praying for you. Will you consider trying church next week? Will you visit some churches and invest yourself in one to find connection?

Let me share one last illustration. Some months ago, my car wouldn't start. I tried several things to fix it and even had the battery checked. I was fearful I was going to be putting out a load of money. I prayed for my car. I looked on Google and YouTube to see if I could find a solution to the problem. A friend told me to check the battery terminals, which I already had done. But I cleaned them thoroughly again and the car cranked up just fine. The moral of the story? I couldn't go anywhere without a good connection.

The same is true for each of us in this life. It's hard to go anywhere unless we have a good connection. Our hearts are longing for meaningful connections. I want you to know that they can be found. I have found them. Friends who have a common faith in Jesus have been a bulwark in the storms of life that have come my way. And I believe this type of friendship is waiting for you.

Notes

Chapter 1 Living Life Alone

1. Anna Fifield, "Cleaning Up After the Dead," *Washington Post*, January 24, 2018, https://www.washingtonpost.com/news/world/wp/2018/01/24/feature /so-many-japanese-people-die-alone-theres-a-whole-industry-devoted-to-clean ing-up-after-them/.

2. Fifield, "Cleaning Up After the Dead."

3. Jim Sliwa, "So Lonely I Could Die," American Psychological Association, August 5, 2017, https://www.apa.org/news/press/releases/2017/08/lonely-die.

4. Ellie Polack, "Cigna's US Loneliness Index Provides Actionable Insights for Improving Body and Mind Health," Cigna, June 17, 2019, https://www.cigna .com/newsroom/news-releases/2019/cignas-us-loneliness-index-provides-action able-insights-for-improving-body-and-mind-health. See also: https://www.cig na.com/assets/docs/newsroom/loneliness-survey-2018-updated-fact-sheet.pdf.

5. Jena McGregor, "This Former Surgeon General Says There's a 'Loneliness Epidemic' and Work Is Partly to Blame," *Washington Post*, October 4, 2017, https://www.washingtonpost.com/news/on-leadership/wp/2017/10/04/this-for mer-surgeon-general-says-theres-a-loneliness-epidemic-and-work-is-partly-to -blame/.

6. Alastair Jamieson, "Britain Appoints 'Minister for Loneliness' to Tackle Social Isolation," NBC News, January 17, 2018, https://www.nbcnews.com/news /world/britain-appoints-minister-loneliness-tackle-social-isolation-n838291.

7. "Loneliness Is a Serious Public-Health Problem," *The Economist*, September 1, 2018, https://www.economist.com/international/2018/09/01/loneliness-is-a -serious-public-health-problem; Amy Novotney, "Social Isolation: It Could Kill You," *Monitor on Psychology* 50, no. 5 (May 2019): 32, https://www.apa.org/mon itor/2019/05/ce-corner-isolation.

8. Bianca DiJulio, Liz Hamel, Cailey Muñana, and Mollyann Brodie, "Loneliness and Social Isolation in the United States, the United Kingdom, and Japan: An International Survey," Kaiser Family Foundation, August 30, 2018, https://www.kff.org/other/report/loneliness-and-social-isolation-in-the-united-states-the-united-kingdom-and-japan-an-international-survey/.

9. "Loneliness Is a Serious Public-Health Problem."

10. "Loneliness Is a Serious Public-Health Problem."

11. "Loneliness Is a Serious Public-Health Problem."

12. "Loneliness Is a Serious Public-Health Problem."

13. María José Carmona, "All the (44 Million) Lonely People," *Equal Times*, August 2, 2018, https://www.equaltimes.org/all-the-44-million-lonely-people#.XmeOwyMpBPY.

14. Carmona, "All the (44 Million) Lonely People."

15. National Institutes of Health, "World's Older Population Grows Dramatically," news release, March 18, 2016, https://www.nih.gov/news-events/news-releases/worlds-older-population-grows-dramatically.

16. "Loneliness Is a Serious Public-Health Problem."

17. Varun Soni, "Op-Ed: There's a Loneliness Crisis on College Campuses," *Los Angeles Times*, July 14, 2019, https://www.latimes.com/opinion/op-ed/la-oe-soni-campus-student-loneliness-20190714-story.html, emphasis added.

18. Joanna Clay, "USC Tackles 'Loneliness Epidemic' in a World of Social Media," *USC News*, December 13, 2018, https://news.usc.edu/152830/loneliness-in-college/.

19. Clay, "USC Tackles 'Loneliness Epidemic.'"

20. Barbara Saddick, "The Loneliness Effect," *US News and World Report*, September 6, 2018, https://www.usnews.com/news/healthiest-communities/articles/2018-09-06/loneliness-the-next-great-public-health-hazard.

21. Quentin Fottrell, "Nearly Half of Americans Report Feeling Alone," MarketWatch, October 10, 2018, https://www.marketwatch.com/story/america-has-a-big-loneliness-problem-2018-05-02.

22. Fottrell, "Nearly Half of Americans Report Feeling Alone."

23. Fottrell, "Nearly Half of Americans Report Feeling Alone."

Chapter 2 It's Hard to Find Someone to Talk To

1. Dan Doriani, *The New Man: Becoming a Man After God's Heart* (Phillipsburg, NJ: P&R Publishing, 2015), 120.

2. "2020 Airbnb Update," Airbnb, January 21, 2020, https://news.airbnb.com/2020-update/.

3. Heather Somerville, "Airbnb's 'Experiences' Business On Track for 1 Million Bookings, Profitability," Reuters, February 13, 2018, https://www.reuters.com/article/us-airbnb-growth/airbnbs-experiences-business-on-track-for-1-million-bookings-profitability-idUSKCN1FX2ZR.

Chapter 3 The Fight against Loneliness

1. Laura Entis, "Scientists Are Working on a Pill for Loneliness," *The Guardian*, January 26, 2019, https://www.theguardian.com/us-news/2019/jan/26/pill-for-loneliness-psychology-science-medicine.

2. Kristine Solomon, "Police Create 'Chat Benches' to Combat Loneliness, Help Make Life a Little Better," Yahoo, June 20, 2019, https://www.yahoo.com/lifestyle/police-create-chat-benches-to-combat-loneliness-help-make-life-a-little-better-210135136.html.

3. Solomon, "Police Create 'Chat Benches' to Combat Loneliness."

4. Solomon, "Police Create 'Chat Benches' to Combat Loneliness."

5. Christopher Dawson, "A Suburbia for the Homeless Exists and They Can Live There Forever," CNN, March 28, 2019, https://www.cnn.com/2019/03/26/us/iyw-town-for-the-homeless-trnd/index.html, emphasis added.

6. "Loneliness Is a Serious Public-Health Problem."

7. Eden David, "Rising Suicide Rates at College Campuses Prompt Concerns over Mental Health Care," ABC News, October 9, 2019, https://abcnews.go.com/Health/rising-suicide-rates-college-campuses-prompt-concerns-mental/story?id=66126446.

8. Clay, "USC Tackles 'Loneliness Epidemic.'"

9. "Loneliness Is a Serious Public-Health Problem."

10. "Loneliness Is a Serious Public-Health Problem."

11. "Loneliness Is a Serious Public-Health Problem."

12. "Loneliness Is a Serious Public-Health Problem."

13. "Loneliness Is a Serious Public-Health Problem."

Chapter 4 Breaking the Pull of Isolation and Insulation

1. "US Adults Have Few Friends—and They're Mostly Alike," Barna, October 23, 2018, https://www.barna.com/research/friends-loneliness/.

2. Mandy Oaklander, "How to Make Friends as an Adult—and Why It's Important," *Time*, February 15, 2018, https://time.com/5159867/adult-friendships-loneliness/.

3. Kaya Burgess, "A Stranger Can Become Your Friend in 90 Hours," *The Times*, April 24, 2018, https://www.thetimes.co.uk/article/a-stranger-can-become-your-friend-in-90-hours-sxtqqvzm0.

4. Mark Leberfinger, "25th Anniversary: Hurricane Hugo Left Path of Destruction in US, Caribbean," Cayman iNews, September 22, 2014, https://www.ieyenews.com/25th-anniversary-hurricane-hugo-left-path-of-destruction-in-us-caribbean/.

5. Kasley Killam, "A Solution for Loneliness," *Scientific American*, May 21, 2019, https://www.scientificamerican.com/article/a-solution-for-loneliness/.

Chapter 5 Fitting In at Starbucks

1. "How Many Starbucks in NYC," Coffee Accessories, September 10, 2019, https://coffeemachinegrinder.com/2019/09/10/how-many-starbucks-in-nyc/.

2. "Our Mission," Starbucks, accessed April 6, 2020, https://www.starbucks.com/about-us/company-information/mission-statement, emphasis added.

3. Susan Haas, "Stop Trying to Fit In, Aim to Belong Instead," *Psychology Today*, October 17, 2013, https://www.psychologytoday.com/us/blog/prescriptions-life/201310/stop-trying-fit-in-aim-belong-instead, emphasis changed.

4. *Merriam-Webster.com Dictionary*, s.v. "unity," accessed April 7, 2020, https://www.merriam-webster.com/dictionary/unity.

5. *Merriam-Webster.com Dictionary*, s.v. "integrity," accessed April 7, 2020, https://www.merriam-webster.com/dictionary/integrity.

6. Scott Kaufman, "Why Inspiration Matters," *Harvard Business Review*, November 8, 2011, https://scottbarrykaufman.com/why-inspiration-matters-harvard-business-review/.

7. Kaufman, "Why Inspiration Matters."

8. Brody Sweeney, "How Starbucks Built a Fortune on the Loneliness of Consumers," *Irish Times*, March 31, 2008, https://www.irishtimes.com/business/how-starbucks-built-a-fortune-on-the-loneliness-of-consumers-1.908511.

Chapter 6 An Imperfect Group of People

1. Ciara Sheppard, "Jennifer Aniston Cries as Young Girl Begs for Help at Christmas," Tyla, February 21, 2020, https://www.tyla.com/entertaining/tv-and-film-jennifer-aniston-ellen-degeneres-show-family-gift-giveaway-kimballs-20191211.

2. Dietrich Bonhoeffer, *Life Together: A Discussion of Christian Fellowship* (New York: Harper & Row Publishers, 1954), 27.

3. Casey McCall, "Why Can't I Find Real Community in the Church?," Prince on Preaching, December 5, 2014, http://www.davidprince.com/2014/12/05/cant-find-real-community-church/.

4. Wendell Berry, *Jayber Crow* (Washington, DC: Counterpoint, 2000), 298.

Chapter 7 The Power of WE

1. Tim Walters, "Moon Landing Made Possible by 400,000 Workers," *USA Today*, July 14, 2019, https://www.floridatoday.com/story/tech/science/space/2019/07/14/moon-landing-made-possible-400-000-workers/1559511001/.

2. Todd Davis, "Why Learning to Think 'We' Not 'Me' Can Help Lead You to Ultimate Success," Thrive Global, January 3, 2018, https://thriveglobal.com/stories/why-learning-to-think-we-not-me-can-help-lead-you-to-ultimate-success/.

3. Davis, "Learning to Think 'We' Not 'Me.'"

4. Davis, "Learning to Think 'We' Not 'Me.'"

5. Davis, "Learning to Think 'We' Not 'Me.'"

6. Ryan Messmore, "The Difference One Church Can Make," The Heritage Foundation, April 1, 2008, https://www.heritage.org/civil-society/report/the-difference-one-church-can-make.

7. Messmore, "The Difference One Church Can Make."

8. Messmore, "The Difference One Church Can Make."

9. Messmore, "The Difference One Church Can Make."

Chapter 8 We Are Family

1. Drew Hunter, "10 Biblical Truths about Real Friendship," Bible Study Tools, October 4, 2019, https://www.biblestudytools.com/bible-study/topical-studies /what-does-the-bible-say-about-friendship.html.
2. Hunter, "10 Biblical Truths."
3. *Merriam-Webster.com Dictionary*, s.v. "fellowship," accessed April 7, 2020, https://www.merriam-webster.com/dictionary/fellowship.
4. *Merriam-Webster.com Dictionary*, s.v. "devote," accessed April 7, 2020, https://www.merriam-webster.com/dictionary/devote.

Chapter 9 Overcoming Roadblocks to Friendship

1. Jodi Easterling-Hood, *Leadership Pros, Woes, and Foes: Companion Guide* (Morrisville, NC: Lulu.com, 2019), 37.
2. "Forgiveness," Sermon Illustrations, accessed April 6, 2020, http://www .sermonillustrations.com/a-z/f/forgiveness.htm.
3. *Lexico*, s.v. "disunity," accessed June 17, 2020, https://www.lexico.com/en /definition/disunity.
4. Matthew Alan Vander Wiele, "An Analysis of Students' Perception of Biblical Community within the Environment of Digital Media: A Mixed Methods Study" (PhD diss., Southern Baptist Theological Seminary, 2014), 49.
5. William Morris, *A Dream of John Ball* and *A King's Lesson* (London; New York; Bombay: Longmans, Green & Co., 1903), 33.

Chapter 10 Learning to Trust

1. Jayson D. Bradley, "What Christians Get Wrong about 'Accountability,'" *Relevant*, October 9, 2017, https://relevantmagazine.com/article/what-christians -get-wrong-about-accountability/.
2. Bradley, "What Christians Get Wrong."
3. Bradley, "What Christians Get Wrong."
4. Bradley, "What Christians Get Wrong."

Chapter 11 The Power of Praying Together

1. Timothy Keller, *Prayer: Experiencing Awe and Intimacy with God* (New York: Dutton, 2014), 23.

Chapter 12 The Joy of Meeting Needs

1. "What Is Stewardship?," Crown, accessed April 7, 2020, https://www.crown .org/blog/what-is-stewardship/.
2. Bible Hub, s.v. *"exagorazó,"* accessed April 6, 2020, https://biblehub.com /greek/1805.htm.
3. Bible Hub, s.v. *"kairos,"* accessed April 6, 2020, https://biblehub.com/str/greek /2540.htm.

Chapter 13 Rally around a Cause

1. "Habitat's History," Habitat for Humanity, accessed April 6, 2020, https://www.habitat.org/about/history.
2. *Merriam-Webster.com Dictionary*, s.v. "corporate," accessed April 6, 2020, https://www.merriam-webster.com/dictionary/corporate.
3. William Temple, *Readings in St. John's Gospel* (London: Macmillan, 1939), 68.

Chapter 15 What Will It Take?

1. 2020 Nissan Altima TV Commercial, "Text Answering," iSpot.tv, https://www.ispot.tv/ad/ZfiP/2020-nissan-altima-text-answering-t1.
2. *Merriam-Webster.com Dictionary*, s.v. "calibrate," accessed April 7, 2020, https://www.merriam-webster.com/dictionary/calibrate.
3. Megan Paraiso, "We Are Better Together," Wave Church, accessed April 6, 2020, https://wavechurch.com/we-are-better-together/.
4. Greg Boyd, "Dismembered: The Church and Individualism," ReKnew, February 2, 2016, https://reknew.org/2016/02/dismembered-the-church-and-individualism/.
5. Paul David Tripp, *Whiter Than Snow: Meditations on Sin and Mercy* (Wheaton: Crossway, 2008), 147.

Chapter 16 You Gotta Have Faith

1. Kelly Seely, "Working Together: How a Shared Gospel Vision Leads to Healthy Partnership in Missions," IMB, August 1, 2017, .https://www.imb.org/2017/08/01/working-together-how-a-shared-gospel-vision-leads-to-healthy-partnership-in-missions/.
2. Seely, "Working Together."

Chapter 17 Encouraging Leaders Who Are Lonely

1. Sarah Zylstra, "Why Pastors Are Committing Suicide," The Gospel Coalition, November 23, 2016, http://resources.thegospelcoalition.org/library/why-pastors-are-committing-suicide.
2. Zylstra, "Why Pastors Are Committing Suicide."
3. Chris Railey, "The Lonely Pastor," *Influence*, May 4, 2018, https://influencemagazine.com/Practice/The-Lonely-Pastor.
4. Railey, "The Lonely Pastor."
5. Railey, "The Lonely Pastor."
6. Josh Reich, "The Weight and Joy of Being a Pastor: Loneliness," ExPastors, http://www.expastors.com/the-weight-and-joy-of-being-a-pastor-loneliness/.
7. Railey, "The Lonely Pastor."
8. Carey Nieuwhof, "Overcoming the New Leadership Epidemic—Isolation and Loneliness," Carey Nieuwhof, June 11, 2018, https://careynieuwhof.com/overcoming-the-new-leadership-epidemic-isolation-and-loneliness/.

Chapter 18 Final Words

1. "Northfield UMC Reaches Community through Free Playtime for Young Children," Minnesota Annual Conference of the United Methodist Church, March 30, 2016, https://www.minnesotaumc.org/itworkeddetail/northfield-umc -reaches-community-through-free-playtime-for-young-children-4267245.

2. "Northfield UMC Reaches Community."

3. "Northfield UMC Reaches Community."

Jack Eason has been the executive director of Crossover CUPS Mission for thirty years. The nonprofit organization's focus is on transforming the lives of young people in the Dominican Republic and Malawi. Additionally, CUPS equips pastors through an annual HONOR event, along with partners such as Focus on the Family and In Touch Ministries. Eason also consults with a variety of nonprofit ministries, helping them develop successful approaches to fund-raising and development. He and his wife, Lynette, have been married twenty-three years and have two children. They live in South Carolina, where they both write, and Jack is blessed to pastor a wonderful group of people at Cross Roads who are genuinely striving to build real connection and community.

GET TO KNOW
JACK

Visit **JACKEASON.ORG** to learn more about Jack's books, blog, speaking, and more!

f jackeasonspeaks

y jackeason

⊙ wjackeason

▶ Jack Eason

JOIN JACK ON A TRIP TO THE DOMINICAN REPUBLIC

and see the impact of the

CROSSOVER CUPS MISSION

Jack spends many weeks a year in the Dominican Republic serving the families and children in the Crossover CUPS program. Come join him on a trip.

For more info on the mission, see

WWW.CUPSMISSION.COM.